PRAISE FOR *TUNED*

"Tuned" chronicles the life lessons learned from a career of fascinating international work experiences while remaining grounded in strong family and personal values. Kevin Cramton's rise to CEO positions details tactics of risk taking and open communication that made him successful. Working together with him was fun and now I know why he made a great executive."

Thomas Stallkamp, former President of Chrysler Corp and DaimlerChrysler Corp.

Wow, if you want to read a very interesting book with a little dose of cars, a healthy dose of Motown music and a very large dose of common sense and advice about family, business and life in general, read "Tuned" by Kevin Cramton. Kevin writes in an easy to read and enjoyable style, and I often found myself stopping to think about what he had written. Kevin's story is the story of adaptation and living the "American Dream" from the rough streets of Detroit to the highest level of business and society.

Randy Foutch, Oil and natural gas entrepreneur, decent cowboy, much better pilot and an avid reader of good books.

Buckle up for a fast ride! Kevin invites us to sit up front for an authentic American success story. His telling offers rich lessons and valuable takeaways, all shared in a spirit of adventure and gratitude. Working with Kevin for years in a public company board room, I've watched him contribute sound judgment, rich wisdom, and insightful guidance that only comes from sitting in the driver's seat. He delivers all that and more to his readers as he shares his deep experience while genuinely prioritizing his faith and family. A rare feat. This is a timely and fun read. Take the road trip!

Hans Helmerich, Chairman of the Board, Helmerich & Payne

Kevin's incredible storytelling ability shines through from the first page, and had me captivated as I anticipated what else he would share about his upbringing and how it influenced his choices and direction his life would take, making him the accomplished person he is today. As he told his story and rolled what he learned into practical and actionable advice on effective leadership, it made me reflect on the excellent experiences we shared while working together at Ford leading the company into the next generation of automotive technology. It was a journey to introduce new powertrain and vehicle technologies and partnerships into Ford's product portfolio, with Kevin bringing his global experiences, business acumen, and keen sense of humor to help us navigate all the challenges. The way he integrated his love of his family into the book is foundational to who he is as a person, and a defining character trait of the person who I am so proud to call my good friend.

MaryAnn Wright, Automotive industry veteran and board director

This is a classic American feel-good story. From the humble beginnings of a Midwest boy from Detroit to the boardrooms in Paris, Tokyo and London, it transcends business — it's ultimately a story about how to live a good life.

Gary Silberg, Retired Partner, Global Head of Automotive, KPMG LLP

"Get Ready" to be entertained and educated, as Kevin relates his life journeys to his experience-learned "four keys to the Dream". You will appreciate and enjoy the healthy doses of insight, inspiration, and motivation; for me, the wide-ranging benefits of (and guidelines for) "taking smart risks" resonated the most. And the introduction (or re-introduction) to the wonders of classic Motown music will be a delightful cherry on the sundae. "Ain't No Mountain High Enough" to keep you from this book!

Mark Malcolm, Former colleague & CEO

Kevin Cramton's successful journey in Corporate America reinforces one of my strong beliefs in life- that if you believe strongly in your mission, you have to embrace a simple concept: to never accept "NO" as an answer. One needs to convert a no to a yes. Kevin's journey embodies my philosophy- a "NO" is a bridge to a "YES". Tuned was that bridge.

Fares Noujaim, Vice Chairman, Guggenheim Partners

Cramton's thrilling account of his journey from the streets of Motown to the boardrooms of Tokyo, Paris, New York, and London is a testament to his strong leadership and commitment to family. Having the opportunity to work with him directly and witness first-hand how he transformed private equity-owned businesses to engineer success and generate great returns for his partners was truly inspiring. Cramton deftly navigated senior positions in expat roles and major domestic corporations. "Tuned" is a must read for anyone in private equity, corporate America, or finance seeking to learn by example how a person can thrive both personally and professionally in any environment.

Michael Duran, Founder, Mill Point Capital

Kevin Cramton's book "TUNED" is an inspiring journey of personal growth and professional success that will resonate with readers from all walks of life.

This captivating memoir captures Cramton's remarkable and engaging story of rising from working-class roots in Detroit to becoming a global business leader, weaving in the rhythms of Motown as a metaphor for life's challenges and triumphs.

The book's four key lessons for leadership and life, illustrated through insightful business and personal examples, will help anyone seeking to learn, grow, and achieve excellence. Part memoir, part leadership guide, and wholly inspiring, "TUNED" is a great read with powerful life lessons!

Michael Meese, Retired General, President, AAFMA

With his humble beginnings, "Tuned" shares Mr. Cramton's keen insights gleaned from years of hard-knock experiences that he accumulated while competing globally against the world's shrewdest bankers. Never losing sight of his strong work ethic or integrity, instilled in him at a young age growing up in the Motor City, he eschews arrogance as he drives home numerous, practical remedies. This book is a delight for anyone, and a special treat, for those fortunate enough to reminisce about simpler days growing up in Detroit. In true, classic modesty, the author recalls a time when he held up the groom in a chair at a wedding. In fact, over the years, it was Mr Cramton who supported the dreams, wishes and future for many who interacted with him. The book "Tuned" will allow many others in the future, to stand tall on his shoulders.

Joel Shulman Ph.D., CFA | Founder/CIO, EntrepreneurShares LLC

This book will grab you and pause the time around you. It gifts you with powerful business and leadership lessons with vignettes gently interspersed between brave life adventures (of a loving family man), whilst delightfully combining local Motown music themes and American lifestyle based around friends, sport and teams. It is equally meaningful across generations, providing life-transforming pearls of wisdom whether facing decisions about what university to attend or running companies. This learning can positively influence creativity and courage. It uncompromisingly pushes you to be fearless and to be an active player who can embrace even failures without losing enthusiasm, and to maintain a curious and explorative mind. It encourages you to strive to achieve your dreams and make an impact on the world.

Dr. Lucia Batty, Physician, London England

In this age of Nepo babies, Kevin Cramton's story can inspire everyone to achieve success in multiple aspects of life, not just the boardroom. As "Dr. K's" creator, I have seen over the last four decades how his hard work, meeting the Redhead and seeking spiritual direction have helped Cramton stay grounded, while attaining success inside the corner office and at home. His accounts and life lessons tell an inspiring story for readers of all ages and backgrounds.

Steve McGowan, Former VP Univision, PBS and Discovery Communications

Kevin Cramton's four ways to become "Tuned" will entertain, inform and inspire, but that's not all. There's a fifth lesson you'll discover when reading about his extraordinary journey with his beloved wife, Faye. Their acts of faith and generosity for family, friends and especially those less fortunate will leave a lasting impression and will be the legacy of this book.

They've been an inspiration for me and I hope you'll discover the same thing. Well done, my friends.

Mark Falkner, The Detroit News, Assistant Sports Editor

Get ready to be inspired as Kevin shares his incredible life journey in this book. Packed with invaluable wisdom and real-life insights, this is a must-read for anyone looking to achieve success in every aspect of life!

Tim Duncan, Successful Industry Executive, Business Consultant, Executive Director Industry Association, and Nonprofit Board Chairman

Kevin Cramton's Tuned inspires us to align our talents and interests, reminding us that trying new things and lifelong learning are crucial to finding the right path for our careers and lives. As a fellow Motown kid and Ford colleague, I can attest that Kevin's leadership lessons are invaluable for anyone seeking to grow both personally and professionally."

Kenneth Behr, Executive Director of Faith Dialogue, friend and former Ford colleague of the author

Tuned is an excellent read and provides important insights into the value of building relationships and smart risk taking. The concepts outlined provide a framework for developing successful relationships and strategies for accessing intelligent risk analysis. The techniques for both topics can be applied on a daily basis through the life journey.

Kevin Bagby, Former Public and PE CFO

Navigating today's dynamic, complex operating environments requires street wisdom, global corporate wisdom, and board wisdom. My friend and colleague, Kevin Cramton, has a stronghold on all three! His work in "Tuned" will deliver a leadership ride that provides humor, heart, and a toolbox of Motown classics to enhance the ride on your leadership road ahead.

Richard S. Lytle, Ph.D., President and CEO, CEO Forum, Inc, Director Emeritus, Lytle Center for Faith and Leadership

I found this book absolutely fascinating as a record of a life well lived, full of hard-won practical experience and smart advice applicable to us all. It's much much more than just another Business Manual. It's a stimulating autobiography of a family man of principle and belief who shares some great global business strategic insights; tracking his personal experiences and philosophy development across the continents and different industries at key junctures in history with some fabled major players. Kevin clearly comes across as a well-respected proven global leader with integrity, energy and a track record of delivery achievement, but who has never forgotten his roots.

John Hitcham, Managing Director, specialist UK based Automotive Consultancy

A must-read for any business leader. Tuned presents captivating, personal, and compelling insights to become a more effective, successful, and transformative business executive.

Matthew Wirgau, Founder and CEO, Midwest Financial M&A.

This book would be an entertaining read for anyone. However, the stories told, and the lessons imparted would be most helpful to someone thinking about where they want to go in life or early in their career.

David Jansen, Past Chairman, National Polish American Sports Hall of Fame

"Tuned" is an inspirational book following the rise from Motown to being involved with international business. Keeping his focus on success in both business and his personal life, he continues his journey to the top of the business world. The vision presented is one that can be followed by individuals seeking to rise in the world of business.

With a blend of humor and Motown music, Kevin shares his journey from his early years to his rise to the top of the business world. Sharing both personal and business stories, he clearly illustrates the keys to success that aspiring executives can follow for success. It can be seen as a reference handbook for future executives.

Tim Lewis, Mayor, Charlotte, MI

Kevin blends tenets of success in life with family antidotes and business strategy that makes for an enlightening journey. It creates a model for others seeking business success and success in life to follow.

Nancy Lewis, First Lady, Charlotte MI

A most incredible book! I love the fact that Kevin made it very clear from the get-go about his faith, and also his incredible relationship with Faye and that she is the cornerstone relationship. That's an amazing thing.

I also love his illustrations throughout the whole of the book. I imagined being on the basketball court when he's talking about having to go home in his bloodied body. All of these experiences on the basketball court helped him to be a very good negotiator, even within the ranks of the car plants in Japan. So many of his younger days in Detroit as a young guy helped him to be the guy he is — Corporate CEO, leading companies, helping companies out of crisis.

I love seeing how our lives had many similarities, Japan, Melbourne, The Beatles; all of this has brought us together as good friends; I'm feeling very privileged that I met him when I did, back in the '90's. I've learned so much from Kevin. I've been mentored, encouraged and I hope that I've encouraged him in my own way. Reading this book has enthused me- I read it from cover to cover without putting it down. I saw so many new things. His wife Faye is Baptist; he's Catholic. My wife was Catholic, I was Baptist but I grew up as a Catholic. We see these interacting lives, and how our life-long partners have been the backbone of everything we've done.

I love the part where Faye asked him to go to the homecoming dance; to see them on that first night out. I've never seen Kevin's hair that long! Amazing. It's been a privilege to be part of the Cramton family life. To marry Claire , baptize Rose — these are highlights of my life. He's a huge sponsor to our church and we are grateful for his sponsorship. I look forward to how this book will be blessed by others, I'm sure they're going to be encouraged, enthused and challenged.

Ian Batty, Reverend, Abbey Road Baptist Church,
London England

TUNED

Copyright © 2024 by Kevin Cramton

All rights reserved.

ISBN (hardback): 979-8-9913718-7-2

ISBN (paperback): 979-8-9913718-6-5

No portion of this book may be reproduced in any form without written permission from the publisher or author, except as permitted by U.S. copyright law.

This publication is designed to provide accurate and authoritative information in regard to the subject matter covered. It is sold with the understanding that neither the author nor the publisher is engaged in rendering legal, investment, accounting or other professional services. While the publisher and author have used their best efforts in preparing this book, they make no representations or warranties with respect to the accuracy or completeness of the contents of this book and specifically disclaim any implied warranties of merchantability or fi tness for a particular purpose. No warranty may be created or extended by sales representatives or written sales materials. The advice and strategies contained herein may not be suitable for your situation. You should consult with a professional when appropriate. Neither the publisher nor the author shall be liable for any loss of profit or any other commercial damages, including but not limited to special, incidental, consequential, personal, or other damages.

hawkeye.pro

Book Cover: Hawkeye

Interior Design: Albatross Book Co.

First edition 2024

TUNED

Leadership Lessons from a Motown Kid Turned Global CEO

KEVIN CRAMTON

FOREWORD		3
INTRODUCTION:	Power Position	5

PART 1: MOTOWN FOUNDATION

CHAPTER 1	The Early Years	19
CHAPTER 2	Change is a Coming	27
CHAPTER 3	That Woman is a Saint	37
CHAPTER 4	Papa's Family Tree	47

PART 2: SHIFTING GEARS

CHAPTER 5	Meeting the Redhead	61
CHAPTER 6	Going off to College	73
CHAPTER 7	Joining Corporate America	79

PART 3: THE INDIANA JONES YEARS

CHAPTER 8	Sumo	97
CHAPTER 9	Americans in Paris	121
CHAPTER 10	All Over the Map	139
CHAPTER 11	Abbey Road	151

PART 4: GOING PRO – THE WORLD OF PRIVATE EQUITY

CHAPTER 12	Flying Around the World	173
CHAPTER 13	Rocky	189
CHAPTER 14	Back Home to Motown	203

CONCLUSION: HIGHER GROUND

CHAPTER 15	View from the Top	219
EPILOGUE	Staying in Tune	229

The Tuned Playlist: A Soundtrack to Stay in the Groove	235
About the Author	237

A SOUNDTRACK TO STAY IN THE GROOVE

Growing up in Detroit in the 60's and 70's was the greatest era for music which continues its worldwide universal appeal—the kind of music that becomes a true soundtrack for life. As I share my journey all through this book you'll find the stories woven together with all-time great songs that complete the picture. I hope you enjoy this compilation—a small gift that holds monumental meaning. The full list is in the back of the book, and this QR code takes you to the Tuned Playlist on my website, with other QR codes for specific songs throughout the book.

TO MY REDHEAD WIFE, FAYE,

who is the sunshine of my life, thank you for your love and support over all these decades.

TO MY CHILDREN, NATHAN, JACK, CLAIRE, AND ROSE,

who experienced both the adventures and disruption of traveling the world and living in different places.

TO MY MOTHER, BEE,

who was my first mentor and biggest cheerleader.

TO MARK, SCOTT, AND DAVID,

who were my first teammates and band of brothers growing up in Motown.

TO MY GRANDCHILDREN,

I hope you are blessed with great relationships, find your calling in life, embrace adventure while taking smart risks, and fully engage the world around you.

FOREWORD

It's an honor to write the foreword for Kevin Cramton's Book *Tuned*. Many business executives feel a desire to share their learnings with others and also want to leave a legacy of memories for their children, grandchildren, and great grandchildren. But few find time or make the effort to do so. Kevin felt it was important to write the story about lessons learned along his journey to share that with others so they and future generations would have a good understanding of what went on before them, and the stories that could have a positive impact on their lives.

Kevin has an amazing memory and did an outstanding job of researching and developing the material that makes this book a wonderful story of navigating change as well as an entertaining explanation of the details and challenges of working overseas for a long time period and the impact it had on their entire family. This material regarding working overseas will be special to people who will be faced with that decision or anyone taking on major changes in life.

The stories he tells about the experiences he and his brothers had growing up in Detroit are not only fascinating but will help others understand what kinds of challenges they faced growing up in an environment of tremendous change. What makes this book special is that it is written not purely from a business point of view but includes how his Christian faith and personal relationships have impacted his life. It not only details Kevin's thoughts and actions but points out the importance of his wife Faye, and the responsibilities and challenges that she dealt with while Kevin was in business activities, and how they balanced the importance of the marriage relationship.

Tuned shows the commitment Kevin and Faye had for the entire family by finding time to be fully engaged in the environment around them, providing the whole family an appreciation of the lifestyles, food, and diversity of the world we live in – which are lessons worth sharing and memories never forgotten.

—DICK SCHULTZ
Olympic and NCAA Leader, Coach, and Mentor

INTRODUCTION
POWER POSITION

The conference table was a long, wooden rectangle, and it was decades old, post-World War II, probably. A little out of place for the sleek, modern offices of Nissan's global headquarters. I looked across it, out the big glass windows that overlooked Yokohama Bay, waiting for a response. Across from me sat a thin, older Japanese man with a full head of dark hair and white shirtsleeves rolled up for the work of negotiation. Nissan's head of purchasing was aggressive and confident, and this was a cut-throat global business. He also needed a cigarette. At some point during our negotiations, his right hand had started shaking; all these guys smoked, and he needed a break. Or maybe his hand was shaking because I had just told him we were out of money, and if things didn't change, he wasn't going to get the parts Nissan needed to make their cars.

The Nissan headquarters are in Yokohama, Japan; it's a big, modern office complex. I was telling my counterpart, who reported to the CEO, Carlos Ghosn, that I needed him to provide us with price increases, or he wasn't going to get any parts, because we were going to go under. By "we," I mean the Japanese parts manufacturer I had been assigned to turn around by my boss, the very wealthy, well-known head of a New York-based Private Equity (PE) firm I joined after my team executed Ford's $15 Billion sale of Hertz in 2005. So, I told Yasuhiro-san that we had put in a lot of money and resources, that I was there to turn this business around, and that I needed his assistance.

Now this was an old-school Japanese businessman, at least 10 years older than me, telling me, "No, no, no." In Japan, you just don't do price increases. It was the same thing with the banks, when we told them we needed concessions on our debt payments. It's not just a business issue, but a "face" issue, meaning that honor is at stake. My right-hand man at the company was also Japanese and had worked in Nissan's orbit for a long time, but he never could have delivered Nissan the straight talk that I could.

When you're a Westerner, especially when you're an American, you get to violate, to some extent, Japanese cultural expectations and roles. You get to be the 6'4" cowboy with the power tie, if you pick your spots right. If I had been Japanese, negotiating with another Japanese executive, we would have had to spend a lot more time doing a whole roundabout dance. They take their time in Japan; it's a consensus society.

But I had to move fast, so I got directly to the point: "Well, then, I guess you don't want any parts." He couldn't have that, and I knew it. Nissan was too dependent on us, they had too much exposure; they couldn't lose such a crucial supplier. We needed them to play ball, but they needed us too. Even though we were on opposite sides of the negotiating table, on different teams, unless we respected each other's strength, it was game over. I learned that almost forty years before, on a backyard basketball court in Motown.

. . .

Growing up in Detroit, basketball was more than a sport; it was culture, entertainment, identity. As a kid, you could establish your worth, learn how to play different roles on a team, see that practice and effort pay off, and experience the immersion of being in the zone; when everything is falling into place.

My brothers and I played outdoor basketball for three out of four seasons a year; only Detroit winters were the off-season. Our first hoop was a cut-out bicycle rim hammered to the garage, but eventually our parents felt sorry for us and got us a backboard, hoop, and nylon net. Compared to the broken-off hoops or bent-down rims with metal nets in our neighborhood, this made our backyard driveway a basketball mecca for our friends, kids we knew who just wanted to hoop, and even future enemies, who would eventually try to steal our bikes, beat us up, and insult my family.

Whenever we dribbled the ball in our backyard, the neighborhood kids showed up after the first couple of bounces. You had to be tough to hang in those games; it was no blood, no foul, get up off the ground, don't bring the weak "stuff" kind of basketball. It was non-stop trash-talk, mind games, anything goes—except for talking about someone's mamma, that got you banned, especially if it was my mamma. During the summer, we played shirts and skins. I don't know if it was an intimidation tactic or just personal hygiene, but no one seemed to cut their fingernails. After an afternoon of playing skins, I looked like I'd been in a knife fight. Mom would almost have to bathe me in hydrogen peroxide. There was no place for weakness on a Motown court, but there was music.

The local guys would bring their portable radios and play Motown and soul music while we played, which was a whole new world for me. The only other music I heard as a kid was the Beatles, because they were on TV with Ed Sullivan. The music of Motown changed my life; it gave me words to put to what was happening all around me, and how I felt about it. It helped me understand and connect with people from different cultures; first with African American kids in urban Detroit, and later, executives from places like Paris, Kyiv, and Tokyo. The way basketball, music, and cars all came together in Detroit helped make us. The creativity, power, and friendships formed during a crazy game of HORSE or an impromptu dunk contest in our backyard mecca, the Jackson 5 ringing through the streets, was something… uniquely American. We learned to connect with people who were different than us, we took risks, we were players in the game, not just spectators. Every time we got up from the ground after a hard foul, we picked up more grit, more perseverance, and the ability to adapt our game to the challenge of the moment. You have to figure out what your best power move is. That's as true on a Motown basketball court as it is in a negotiating room in Yokohama.

. . .

It turns out, in both Motown basketball and Japanese negotiation, insults are an art form. In Japan, insults are inflicted by trying to shame people for failure, and make them cower, which is expressed through stern words and disapproving body language. Both the Nissan negotiator and the bank tried to use that cultural shame strategy, which worked on my Japanese teammates but was totally ineffective on a Motown kid who grew up with way worse.

On the flip side, threats and acting like a "cowboy" had to be choreographed at the right time to be effective, or people would just tune out. Threats were only effective if you had the ability and will to carry them out. It was only after they knew I wasn't bluffing, and realized the impact it would have on them, that they got serious and gave us what we needed. In the end, they respected our tenacity and the power position we were in.

That story has a happy ending, even though it also ultimately involved multiple negotiations, months of critical decision-making on the ground, flying around the world more times than I can count, an earthquake and tsunami that almost turned into the worst nuclear disaster since Chernobyl, and an exit deal that almost didn't go through. We'll get back to all of that, because it was one of the biggest challenges I've ever faced, and overcoming it took everything I had learned over the four previous decades. Those lessons from my family, in college and early business, decades of marriage and raising children, traveling the world for Ford Motor Company, living as an American in places like France, the United Kingdom, and Japan, and cutting Billion-dollar deals while running multiple companies in the world of private equity helped me see the bigger picture more clearly. That bigger picture is a story of the pursuit of a well-tuned life; of becoming someone who can make adjustments, adapt, and successfully navigate the world around you. Those lessons, it turns out, are the keys to the American Dream, and for me, it was all built in Motown.

PART 1

MOTOWN FOUNDATION

Growing up in Motown, I learned four key lessons that were fundamental for my personal and professional growth. On my journey from the humble beginnings of a working-class family in Detroit to becoming a global business executive and CEO, these keys helped me pursue—and live out—the American Dream. After having traveled, worked, and lived around the world, I have found this Dream to be close to universal in scope.

Think of these as the four ways to become *tuned*: Someone who can adapt, make adjustments, and successfully navigate the world around you. These keys will pave the way for any leader to drive towards their Dream:

Find Points of Connection, Pursue Alignment, Take Smart Risks, and Be a Player.

I. **FIND POINTS OF CONNECTION:** Personal relationships are critical to your success. Your ability to effectively connect with others, both personally and professionally, will be critical in developing the friendships and mentoring relationships that are key to achieving your dreams—because no one does it alone. Strong relationships are foundational for the mental, physical, and spiritual development that are necessary to build both your and your team's potential, in every area of your life.

The most important relationship decision is choosing a good partner to share your journey. Life can be challenging, and having a great partner to take on the world is key. Strong partnerships and personal relationships are the building blocks to a meaningful life and the pursuit of happiness.

Aside from finding your life partner, intentionally invest in other deep relationships. Be discerning about who you spend your time with. Build positive relationships where there is mutual benefit and growth. The people you surround yourself with greatly influence your life—so choose wisely. Having good friends and mentors who can provide honest feedback and hold you accountable is critical.

Investing in personal relationships builds the relational capital that can be utilized in good times and bad, to accomplish extraordinary things—both in an organization and in your personal life. Developing relational capital usually starts with identifying a *point of connection* that you can build from. A true partnership requires teamwork, trust, and a mutual ongoing effort to be successful.

2. **PURSUE ALIGNMENT:** Continually explore opportunities that test you, encourage growth, and help you to *align your talents and interests*. Trying and learning new things should be a lifelong pursuit. This is especially critical when determining which path to pursue regarding your vocation (or career). To make sure your future decades are enjoyable, first determine the best combination of what you enjoy and are very good at when discerning your vocation. Getting this right will save you a lot of time and money.

Some people say, "Do what you love," but that is too simple a formula to get you where you are trying to go. I love basketball, played on the high school team, and even scored thirty-five points in a game, but in reality, I was not even in the same universe as the guys I knew who ended up playing professionally. So even though I loved basketball, it was not a viable career path. Enjoying something is not the only criterion to consider when choosing a career. Your interests have to *align* with your talents and what the world needs.

Because of this, it is critical to test and match what you enjoy with what you can be good at professionally. Clearly assess your skills and potential vocation and career matches to determine if that is a field you enjoy. Too often, people confuse a strong interest or passion for a basis for a career when it might be better suited for a hobby or an outside-of-work endeavor.

It can be difficult to determine if you will enjoy something, especially without experiencing or trying it firsthand over a period of time. Trying different things not only helps you grow but is critical to finding the best fit for you. Talk to people who work in your area of interest, look for potential mentors, see if you can shadow them at work, volunteer, or try part-time jobs or internship opportunities to see how people operate in the real world—like a test drive of a car before you buy it. Given that you are likely to have multiple careers, vocations, and professional interests during life, you should be constantly *test-driving* new things. These principles are not just for young people trying to choose a career or vocation, but for all those looking for a new path or the next adventure.

3. **TAKE SMART RISKS:** Smart risks are thought-through and calculated action plans to make sure the reward is greater than the risk—and that the risk will not be catastrophic if you fail. Pursue opportunities that may have a risk of failure or of coming up short but are good learning experiences, stretch you either professionally or personally, or might provide a stepping stone to further advancement or development. Develop a process that includes analyzing the benefits and risks, seeking wise counsel, and leaning on spiritual guidance from trusted sources.

For me, my early grounding in discerning smart risks came from growing up on the streets of Detroit, where this type of awareness and approach was necessary for survival.

Success in pursuing your dreams will mean getting out of your comfort zone. This does not come naturally, and you will need to make a conscious decision to do it. But if you do, you'll differentiate yourself from others and position yourself for a wider range of opportunities. In both everyday life and in the marketplace, selecting which risks to take gets easier with experience and thoughtful analysis, though no approach is ever perfect.

Learning from the successes of others, and especially their failures, is a game-changer. Mentoring relationships are a great way to improve streamlined decision-making and hone your approach to improving your chances of success. Once you take on a smart risk, periodically assess the results and apply the learnings from that assessment to improve your chances of success over time.

4. **BE A PLAYER:** Choose to be fully engaged in the present moment and the world around you; be a player, not a spectator in life. Be an active participant in every facet of your life. Technology can make this a challenge for us today. The advent of the internet, online gaming, social media, virtual reality, the digital metaverse, and AI can tempt you to become a spectator in life, distanced from real-world relationships, with the risk of being disconnected and distracted as the world around you passes you by.

Although this challenge is greater today, it has always been an issue and can be the primary reason why many people don't reach their potential and fail to achieve their dreams. Achieving your dreams takes engagement and hard work over a long period of time. There are no shortcuts or painless paths. The support of a good network of friends and mentors who encourage you to keep going will pave the way for long-term success.

Over one hundred years ago, Theodore Roosevelt captured this concept well in a commencement address at the Sorbonne in Paris titled "Person in the Arena." When we talk about the arena, you might think of the Gladiators in the Roman Coliseum, or "Rocky" in the boxing ring, but we all have the opportunity to engage in the arena of life—competing and striving to achieve our dreams.

He talked about the choice we all make to either be in the arena as an active participant in life, or to go through life as a spectator, sitting on the sidelines:

"It is not the critic who counts; not the person who points out how the strong man stumbles, or where the doer of deeds could have done them better. The credit belongs to the person who is actually in the arena, whose face is marred by dust and sweat and blood; who strives valiantly; who errs, who comes short again and again, because there is no effort without error and shortcoming; but who does actually strive to do the deeds; who knows great enthusiasms, the great devotions; who spends themselves in a worthy cause; who at the best knows in the end the triumph of high achievement, and who at the worst, if they fail, at least fails while daring greatly, so that their place shall never be with those cold and timid souls who neither know victory nor defeat."

Are we really living without being in the arena, fully engaged, participating in the world around us? In my experience, I've found that you need to get in the arena, choose to be a participant and not a spectator in life, invest in relationships, continuously try new things, take smart risks, and keep pursuing the dream to your full potential.

As I take on each day's challenges, these four keys are non-negotiable for me to achieve a successful outcome. The following chapters (1-4) chronicle these key lessons I learned from my foundational experiences in Motown, which were refined through the transition periods of high school, college, and entering the corporate world, sharpened during our adventure years of working around the world, then deployed at the highest level as I was "going pro" by moving to the professional sports-style world of private equity (PE).

Some say the Dream is not attainable any longer, that people are not going to have the opportunities that previous generations had. I do not believe that is true—in fact, it is just the opposite. The opportunities are boundless. The key is to be prepared for the pursuit. The Declaration of Independence speaks of the unalienable rights of life, liberty, and the pursuit of happiness —to me, this is the meaning of the Dream.

In my life, I have had the opportunity to either work, live in, or visit about fifty countries around the world. All of them have interesting people, unique cultures, and their own kind of greatness, but absolutely none provide opportunities like we have in America, especially for individuals from working-class backgrounds, to raise themselves out of humble beginnings through hard work, perseverance, and grit, to achieve their dreams.

Part One of this book, Motown Foundation, highlights the formative impact that growing up in Motown had, not only on me, but also my brothers, my parents, and even our grandparents and great-grandparents before us. Like many others from all over the world over the past century, my family viewed Detroit as a beacon of new opportunities and a place for pursuing your Dream.

Since I literally grew up in Detroit, where I first learned these keys, formed and surrounded by Motown music, I've assembled a Tuned playlist that helps provide a theme for each chapter and highlight the life experiences that still resonate with me as I drive toward the Dream of a well-tuned life. I hope this helps you enjoy the ride.

CHAPTER 1

THE EARLY YEARS

"ABC" - JACKSON 5

As a young kid growing up in Motown, I began to learn key skills that would later help me navigate life's adventures. It might seem obvious, but reading, writing, and arithmetic skills would be, for me, critical to success in achieving the Dream. Just as important in shaping me, though, was the city itself.

I was born at Fort Belvoir in Alexandria, Virginia, when my father was in the Army. My mother liked to tell people that I was a very inexpensive acquisition, costing only six dollars—apparently the bill for the hospital food. After completing his military service, my father and his young family returned to his native Michigan and the City of Detroit, where my parents had both been born. We lived in a rented two-story flat with my family on the first floor and my father's parents and sister on the second floor. This was *a lot* of togetherness—especially for my mother.

Detroit has a long history, founded in 1701 by French explorer Antoine de la Mothe Cadillac and located in a strait linking two of the Great Lakes. Two hundred years after the city's founding, General Motors adopted the "Cadillac" name as its flagship luxury brand. In the middle of the Twentieth Century, Detroit was experiencing, as in Dickens' *A Tale of Two Cities*, "the best of times" and "the worst of times." In the 1960's, Detroit had a lot going for it. The US auto industry was still enjoying its post-war dominance, launching vehicles like the iconic Mustang, and muscle cars ruled the streets. Ford was beating Ferrari at Le Mans, and the market share of the Big Three automakers was a virtual monopoly.

Detroit was truly the world's Motor City, or as some of the locals called it: Motown. For over a decade after World War II, Detroit, riding the auto boom, was the richest city in the world, boasting the highest per capita income. Unfortunately, this turned out to be the calm before the storm.

Our neighborhood in Northwest Detroit was mostly working class but was also home to a number of professional athletes (back when most had off-season jobs to get by), Motown singers, and our down-the-street neighbor, union leader Jimmy Hoffa. I didn't know who Hoffa was, but he was clearly special, riding in the back of a luxury car when most of the neighbors drove Fords, Chevys, or Dodges. Only later, while watching movies on Hoffa, did I realize that this was a family whose kids we played with on a regular basis.

One of the indelible experiences in those early years was growing up surrounded by the sounds of Motown music. It is amazing that music, especially in your youth, can act as a lifelong marker that brings back memories and experiences every time you hear a certain tune. Motown Music was founded in Detroit the year I was born by Berry Gordy Jr., a former Ford factory worker, who received a loan from his family to start the company. The Motown sound was a combination of soul and popular music, which gave it a unique crossover appeal to a broad audience spanning race, gender, and social status. Many of the early artists were from Detroit, including several who grew up singing gospel songs at local churches. Berry Gordy applied some of the production concepts and disciplines from his Ford experience to create a real music factory. In the early years, Motown music, like the city itself, was booming.

Every experience during those days living in Detroit, and even beyond, seems to be anchored in my memory by a Motown song. My go-to playlist is always Motown, not just in Detroit, but everywhere I've traveled and lived around the world. One of my greatest joys as a parent has been sharing that love of Motown music with my kids. One of my best Father's Day gifts was at the Motown Museum with my youngest daughter. We were standing in the recording studio, in the exact place David Ruffin stood when he sang "My Girl," our special song. It doesn't get any better than that. Throughout my journey, I've often connected a Motown song to each landmark experience, given the unique place of Motown music in my life, and the universal language those songs seem to speak.

I was the oldest of four boys, separated by only five years from top to bottom. Our household was a constant wrestling match. As time went on, we became closer and spent a lot of time together. To survive in Detroit, my brothers and I had to stick together and defend and protect each other —we always had each other's backs. We were a band of brothers that were raised on the streets of Detroit, and that has endured for all the decades since.

Given that I was the oldest of the four, I was the de facto leader and in many cases the trailblazer, which helped make me who I am today. On the other hand, my youngest brother, Dave, had the advantage of seeing everyone go before him—plus my parents tired out over time. Mark and Scott had the advantages and disadvantages of being middle children.

We did everything together; playing, fighting, eating, and even sleeping with all four of us in the same bedroom for a while. I naturally paired up with my brother Mark (or "Sharky," as he came to be known from his swimming exploits) who was sixteen months younger than me, while our two younger brothers, Scott and David, paired up. Mark was my match, so we initially shared a bed together, later were roommates, we played on sports teams together, and he was the best man at my wedding. Growing up with my brothers was a great early lesson in team play and how to get along with others.

Growing up as a band of brothers in Detroit, especially during this time of transition, was like being in a laboratory, testing and experimenting with what I would later realize were the four keys to the Dream: Finding points of connection, pursuing alignment, taking smart risks, and being a player. One of the best teachers for learning these key lessons is sports. Although I'm the only brother who did not end up pursuing a teaching and coaching career, we all learned from playing sports. I do wonder sometimes, especially when we compare our golf games, who took the better path.

Powered by all those sugary products we ate as kids, we had boundless reserves of energy, so we tried a lot of things, including almost every sport you can imagine: Baseball, basketball, football, ice and field hockey, tennis, golf, running, bowling, curling, croquet, horseshoes, boxing, wrestling, volleyball, badminton, biking, sword fighting, and my favorite, Kung Fu fighting with nunchucks (thanks to Bruce Lee).

"Necessity is the mother of invention," so when the four of us wanted to play hockey, we had to improvise. Even in "Hockeytown," during those cold Michigan winters, with little money nor access to facilities or equipment, we had to be creative and enterprising to be able to play. My mother bought us a long roll of thick plastic that we used to line the bottom of our backyard to create the base for an ice rink. The banks of the rink were made from compacted snow. It was an engineering wonder, considering that it was built by a bunch of elementary school kids. We filled the rink with a hose attached to the basement wash tub that weaved its way up through a window. Did it create a cold draft in the house and likely run up the heating bill? Yes. But it worked.

Since we didn't have the money for new skates or sticks, we turned to second-hand stores for skates and friends' garages and basements for old sticks. We learned firsthand that shoe polish and sharpening could make the skates serviceable, while we became experts in taping sticks to keep them together. Unfortunately, we couldn't find a goalie stick, so a bat had to suffice, which made the goaltender a dangerous defender. As we pretended to be members of the Red Wings, this simple but creative set of solutions enabled us to enjoy those cold, cloudy Michigan winters—and got us out of the house, to our parents' relief.

The Kung Fu craze that was brought about by Bruce Lee led us to design, build, and decorate our own nunchucks. We cut old broomsticks to the right size, taped the handles to get personalized grips, and attached the pieces with small chains and winged screws. With a little paint for the Chinese symbols, we were ready for Kung Fu Fighting. Fortunately, those fights only resulted in minor injuries.

My foray into tennis was an unexpected turn for a kid living in Detroit. Tennis, at that time, and to this day, was a rich person's sport. To reach a high level, it requires professional training, access to indoor facilities, and the ability to play constantly, including tournaments—all expensive endeavors. The US Tennis authorities appeared to recognize this lack of economic diversity and started a program in the early 1970s called the National Junior Tennis League (NJTL), which focused on getting less affluent and inner-city kids into tennis. They provided rackets, balls, professional instruction, and some access to indoor training in the winter. My mother heard about this program and signed me and my brothers up immediately—more to give her some free time than out of a pure love for tennis.

Doing something for the first time is usually awkward, but with practice and good instruction, my brothers and I started to excel. We began to compete against players from other places, and our site team won the city championship. As a novice player, I competed and won my local division in the Detroit News Tennis Tournament for my age group. I continued playing, including using indoor facilities during the winters that were sponsored by the NJTL. I became good enough to play as a freshman on my high school team.

Eventually, I concluded that reaching the next level required a focused commitment to tennis (forgoing my other sports interests) and significant financial resources my family simply didn't have. Despite this, tennis has become a lifelong sport for me. I never thought as a young player that this was something I would enjoy for life, nor did I imagine, as a Detroit kid, that my future business career would enable me to attend all four Grand Slam events in Melbourne, Paris, London, and New York.

All these experiences were great for teamwork, skill building, and active life engagement—including early entrepreneurial and problem-solving opportunities that developed skills I have used throughout my business career, from start-ups to turnarounds. Life is full of unexpected avenues along the journey. Trying new things is part of taking smart risks that enable you to begin to understand where your interests and talents align. As kids, we didn't think about how all those sports activities would end up resulting in certain career choices; especially for my three brothers, who all became high school coaches and gym teachers. At one time, I considered the same path, but as I was exposed to business and the marketplace, I found a better alignment of my interests and skills. This didn't mean I gave up my passion for sports; instead, I channeled it into recreational activities, building relationships, and later, coaching my kids. Whether it was sports, music, my family, or the city itself, I'll always be grateful for the ABCs and 123s of my Motown foundation.

CHAPTER 2
CHANGE IS A COMING

"A BALL OF CONFUSION" - TEMPTATIONS

The late 60s and early 70s were a time of great social and economic change. From a new, more global economy (and competition) to civil rights, the make-up of Detroit was rapidly transforming as middle-class whites departed for the suburbs. My family remained in the city, and we experienced firsthand the consequences of these changes—some good and some bad.

In 1967, one of the deadliest and largest riots helped precipitate a catastrophic fall for one of the world's greatest cities. The Detroit Riots began on July 23 and lasted through July 28, and were the bloodiest urban uprisings in the US until the LA Riots in the early 90s.

I was a young kid, but I remember that time vividly. Our house in Detroit was a few miles south of 8 Mile Road, later made famous by rapper Eminem, and not far from the National Guard Armory, where we watched the troops and armored personnel carriers travel down the main street of our neighborhood. My father, an ex-Army soldier, slept in the front room of the house with his loaded rifle. Through our TV we watched in shock as an urban war raged just miles away.

The 1967 Riots catalyzed the migration of middle-class families to the suburbs, and as most of our previous neighbors departed, we began to nervously welcome new neighbors. One of the first African American families to move in was the Scotts. They were a professional couple with no kids. Mr. Scott worked at Hostess, and he taught an important lesson to my brothers and me on how to build relationships with very different people through points of connection. He provided an abundant supply of day-old Twinkies, Ho Hos, Ding Dongs, and Fruit Pies—to my siblings, he was the Black Willy Wonka. We loved the Scotts, even if they were a new kind of family; they liked Twinkies just like us.

One of our other neighbors, Kathy, was a single African American woman with no children in her mid-thirties. She drove a relatively new car and dressed for work in office attire, which was an anomaly for the neighborhood. Kathy always reminded me of the American film star Pam Greer.

Our houses were only about 10 feet apart, so we saw Kathy often. From time to time, she would ask my mother for help to handle deliveries and to watch over things when she couldn't be home. She was the only person I knew who called my mother by her given first name, Elizabeth. My mother had gone by Betty since she was a kid, but Kathy was formal and polite. My mother and Kathy were around the same age and seemed to get along despite their fundamentally different backgrounds.

I will never forget the concert Kathy hosted in her backyard one warm, summer night. The band set up a large stage in the backyard with a speaker system that would rival a professional concert venue. As my family watched the set-up, I could tell my parents were nervous about what was about to happen. As the afternoon turned into evening, the guests began to arrive, dressed to the nines, as if they were going to a fancy event. Then the music began, and our house started shaking from the reverberation of the speakers.

My brother and I were sharing a basement bedroom with a perfect view of the stage and all the interesting people pouring in. The "concert" seemed to go on for hours, and we got up to an unofficial count of over two hundred attendees. Even the police came by to see what was happening but chose not to engage the crowd and went on their way.

This was my first concert and party, and it exposed me to the performances and music I would soon come to love. After the concert was over, my parents never talked about it again, but to us kids it was a cultural awakening. This  culture, although radically different from our own, produced something that was beautiful and relatable. I learned that finding that point of connection, like a love for The Temptations, Martha Reeves, or other Motown acts, was a surefire way of building bridges. Music was a universal language. Martha Reeves, who was my all-time favorite female Motown artist, said that this music was great at crossing over barriers to bring people together.

As I mentioned before, basketball, and the friendships it fostered, was another entry point. The backyard games with neighborhood kids of all kinds, the trash talk and rough style of play, the battle scars, the Motown music playing in the background, the creative HORSE games and dunk competitions—all of it added up to a point of connection that helped us build all kinds of relationships across racial and other boundaries, and it changed my life for good. While sports can build inroads between young people, they can also function as a foundation for the entire community to come together. I know of no better example than the 1968 Detroit Tigers, who seemed to rally everyone around the American League baseball Pennant race, and ultimately, a World Series Championship. This Championship run was only a short time after the riots that took place the prior year not far from the Stadium, and it was surprising to see so much communal cohesion in such a divided time.

The Tigers had an excellent team, including several African American players. One of them was a local high school talent named Willie Horton, a young muscular power hitter and a fan favorite. His story was one of hope and success, a hometown champion actually "making it." After the Tigers won the Series, everyone was dancing in the streets.

Not everything about the radical changes in Detroit was as positive as backyard concerts and baseball championships. Our neighborhood became more dangerous over time, with crime and drugs becoming an ongoing problem. We found out that some people did not like us just because of our skin color. My brothers and I were some of the few white kids in our classes in the Detroit Public Schools we attended, and we faced verbal and physical abuse from other students almost daily. Teachers tried to manage the classrooms, but little learning was taking place amidst the chaos.

I was called every white racial epitaph and, to survive, tried to deflect or ignore it. At one point I embraced the nickname "Casper," a reference to the very friendly (and very white) ghost. This was by far the best choice from a list of other alternatives. I became skilled in deflecting these jabs and dismissive nicknames while pressing forward and learned how to take it in stride—a lesson I utilized for the rest of my life.

Although my brothers and I took a lot of the abuse, my Black friends were belittled by others in class because of their association with me. There also was little respect for discipline or authority, and I experienced firsthand, as a member of the safety patrol, that not everyone respected you, and gangs went out of their way to abuse those who served in those roles.

From these experiences, I discovered that there were three types of relationships, the first and most valuable being those deep friendships that feature closeness, undying loyalty, and long-term sustainability—these are as rare as precious jewels. Everyone needs this level of deep relationships to provide support, advice, and comfort as you navigate through life.

The second type is mutual relationships, in which you share a common bond with another person, but that bond can be quickly challenged by tough circumstances. These are casual relationships and can end as quickly as they come. I've been disappointed by "fair weather" friends many times in my life, often because I thought the relationship was deeper than it truly was.

The last type is a "transactional" relationship, which revolves around a mutual interest, circumstance, or exchange, and is, by nature, limited and fleeting. When we were hosting hoops, we played with everyone in the neighborhood, but quickly learned the difference between good friends and the people who just wanted to play. This was most evident when we found a group of guys in our garage attempting to steal our bikes after a game. The surprising thing was that there was no remorse but just regret that they were caught.

This reminds me of the Biblical parable of building a house. You can build it on sand, like with transactional relationships which have no real basis and are by nature unstable. You can build it without strong foundations, like with fair-weather friends who have conditional loyalty based on shared interests. Finally, you can build your home on rock, where it is solid and strong, like with those deep, meaningful friendships. Understanding the various types of relationships is one of the keys to a successful personal and professional life—no matter the context, whether the boardroom or the dinner table, you will always have to navigate these different kinds of relationships. Contrary to popular belief, relationships require investment and effort. Learning to invest enough in lasting relationships, versus overinvesting in transactional relationships, is critical, and getting the balance wrong is a common mistake.

My early experiences in Motown also taught me that people have two choices when confronted with a problem: Engage and actively address the difficult situation or surrender and cloister yourself away from potential danger. I realized early that I wanted to take the first option, and part of being engaged with your problems is understanding smart risks.

As our neighborhood became more dangerous, my family had to learn how to navigate our community without putting ourselves into bad situations. This made activities more carefully planned, which increased the chances of success but reduced spontaneity. I have found this approach, with its inherent tradeoffs, a successful strategy in both personal and professional situations: We aim to improve our chances of success while reducing the risk of catastrophic failure.

Although we spent time and effort planning our "smart risks," there is still no guarantee that everything would go as planned. On one occasion, my family developed a tactical strategy to acquire sugar-and-salt-laden snacks from the local party store. While most people consider getting snacks a mild inconvenience at worst, we were dealing with a local gang who controlled the entrance to the store, usually shaking down and harassing kids trying to enter or exit. My brothers and I experienced this harassment firsthand and decided to put a plan in place to get the Faygo sodas, barbeque chips, and licorice we craved.

The first step was reconnaissance missions to determine the patrol patterns of the gang members near the store entrance just around the corner from our house. After determining the optimal time for the mission, we had to select our courier, who would exchange our money for delectable delights and transport those back to the safety of our house. After much deliberation, the choice became clear: Our youngest brother Dave, who was the fastest and smallest of us all, would be drafted into our snack operation.

We launched the mission in the early afternoon, and everything seemed to be going to plan. After about ten minutes, we saw Dave sprinting around the corner carrying a bag and we started to cheer. We then saw multiple gang members turn the corner in fast pursuit, trying to cut him off. As he tried to pick up the pace, one of his gym shoes flew off, but his survival instincts kept him running for the sanctuary of the house. The gang members retrieved his shoe and offered to trade it for our goods, but we refused. Once it was clear we would not trade, they threw his shoe on the roof of the store, which we believe still lies there to this day.

It was a bittersweet experience; we got the prize we wanted (snacks) but it came at an unexpected cost, and this is true for most decisions in life. Unfortunately, being engaged in the "arena" and taking risks sometimes carries a cost. With experience and understanding, you get better at the process of risk-taking. After our foray into the store, we improved our planning and intelligence gathering, moving around the neighborhood like ninjas, and we rarely got detected or caught in the wrong position again.

Although we got more sophisticated in trying to stay safe, the advent of events like "Devil's Night" in Detroit made balancing safety and opportunity more challenging. Unfortunately, our house became a target as time went on, being hit with rocks and bottles by some of the local kids. One "Devil's Night," my father made a major error in judgment and parked our second car, an old Dodge, on the street. We woke up early that next morning to the car on fire.

Although you had to watch out for the gangs, the true danger was the neighborhood dogs. At that time, there seemed to be only four types of dogs: Pitbulls, Dobermans, German Shepherds, and Rottweilers. Unfortunately, from time to time they would get loose or run in packs, prowling the streets just looking for trouble. There were plenty of times when our speed and tree-climbing abilities were put to the test. My brother Scott demonstrated his best athletic capabilities going up the trees when the dogs were chasing him.

Growing up in Detroit was a practical kind of education, where I began to learn the importance of relationships, trying new things, managing smart risks, and staying engaged in the world around me. I learned to be resilient in the face of challenges, from bullying to gang violence, and realized that you must decide each day to get in the game and push forward—or disengage and sit on the sidelines too paralyzed to move.

CHAPTER 3

THAT WOMAN IS A SAINT

"REACH OUT (I'LL BE THERE)" - FOUR TOPS

My mother spent her life supporting my brothers and me, meeting our physical, mental, and spiritual needs, not only when we were kids, but throughout our lives. She was always there for us and put our needs sacrificially ahead of hers. She personified the four keys to the Dream and helped us live them out as we grew older.

Mom was a second-generation Polish American. Both her parents' families came through Ellis Island in the late 1800s to pursue the American Dream. As a kid, I got to spend time with my grandparents, especially my grandmother's family, the Kobus's. My great-grandparents came to America as adults and moved several times between the Midwestern Polish enclaves of Milwaukee, Chicago, and Detroit. My great-grandfather was a talented musician and organ master. He was recruited from

Chicago in the late 1890s to be the organist at the newly built European-style Gothic church, the Sweetest Heart of Mary, built with the nickels and dimes of the Polish immigrants making a life in Detroit. These immigrants aimed to create a magnificent cathedral to remind them of the best of their native Poland. The church was constructed using the very best materials available, including award-winning stained-glass windows from the 1893 Columbian exhibition in Chicago and a large Austin pipe organ, the oldest electro-pneumatic organ in Michigan.

Once I was visiting the church after a Lenten Friday fish fry and mentioned that my great grandfather was the first church organist. My brother and I were offered an impromptu tour upstairs to see the organ. It reminded me of climbing the stairs of a great European cathedral, and when reaching the summit, we saw this magnificent piece of art. We asked if we could sit at the organ keyboard, where my great-grandfather played over one hundred years before; what a privilege to have this opportunity to sit in the same seat as our great grandfather—the organ master!

When my great-grandfather took the position with the church, the family was able to secure a loan to buy a house on Russell Street, a block from the church, with a storefront, rear living quarters, two upper flats, a large attic, outhouse, and a carriage house with a brick alley for the horses. The house was built in the 1890s, before indoor toilets and electricity—which were added years later. This was Detroit before it was known for the automobile.

As my great-grandfather was working at the church, my great-grandmother became an entrepreneur running the family store, which was part general goods and part religious goods and school supplies for the church and school. She was also responsible for renting out the two upper flats, while maintaining the household and being the mother of eight children. Although they encountered personal and financial challenges during their lives, here was a quintessential, successful immigrant family, pursuing their American Dream.

Some people say those immigrant success stories are a thing of the past, that these opportunities no longer exist. I think the opposite is true, and that this is the best time for those in America who want to work hard to pursue their Dreams.

While traveling around the country, I usually chat with my cab or Uber drivers, who are often immigrants, to learn about their stories. One of my drivers, who had come to the US from Ethiopia over 10 years ago, had a new Lincoln, and given that I worked for Ford for years, I was interested in how he liked his car. He told me this was his second Lincoln, and after driving and working other jobs for years, he owned it outright.

He also told me that he owned a *brick* house, an interesting way of describing your home to a stranger. He explained that poorer people from his country lived in houses made from sticks and dung, while the rich people lived in houses made from cinder blocks—but he lived in a brick house, better than anything even rich people had in his country of origin. He was living the Dream.

After my great-grandparents passed, my Aunt Helen took over the role of running the store and household while my Uncle Al became the primary family provider from his wages as a delivery driver for the Stroh Brewery. Except for my grandmother and the eldest son, the other four adult kids never married and spent their lives in the family home. My Aunt Helen was a kind and generous woman with a gentle spirit. She was a very religious woman, attending church daily, spending her life in service to others, and was fervent in her prayer life—a great role model of a Christian woman. It was clear that my mother loved her; we used to visit every other week, and really enjoyed spending time with her. Aunt Helen knew the power of relationships, and that food was a great point of connection for me and my brothers, so when we spent time together, we usually ended up at Burger King by the end of the day.

Unlike my aunt, my grandmother did get married, and for the first several years lived in one of the upstairs apartments. My mother and her older sister were born while the family still lived in that apartment. The combination of needing more space and my grandfather tiring of living with his in-laws saw them move into a rental in a Polish neighborhood on the west side of Detroit, where my grandparents lived until their passing. My mother was close to her father, and they became "buddies" as she grew older. On the other hand, she had a respectful, but at times strained, relationship with her disciplinarian mother.

My grandfather worked at Dodge Main, one of the largest auto plants for what was then the Chrysler Corporation (now Stellantis). Although the plant was in the then-predominantly Polish American city of Hamtramck, it was clearly best for advancement in the company if your name looked and sounded American. Because of this, he had his name changed to Roth from the very Polish and hard-to-spell and pronounce Ratajczak. Interestingly, my mother and her sister, who lived in a neighborhood and attended Catholic schools with mostly Polish American kids, retained their Polish surname. Although he never smoked, my grandfather eventually contracted lung cancer, likely from exposure at the plant, and died in his early sixties—which greatly impacted my mother.

After graduating high school, my mother went to work in a professional job as a bank teller in the neighborhood while she continued to live at home. She met my father at a dance for young adults, they dated for a few years and then were married. My father, who grew up with no religious upbringing, converted to Catholicism to marry my mother. Shortly after they were married, my father was drafted into the Army, and he and my mother headed off to Fort Belvoir in Virginia.

While my father was stationed in the army, my mother worked at the local bank to supplement the family income. Given that Alexandria at the time was still very much a Southern town, it was not easy for the Army wives, especially a Yankee like her, to find a position. But my mother was persistent, and because she had previous experience as a bank teller, was able to secure a position—and stayed in that role until a little before my birth.

Within a year after moving South, I was born at the Army hospital, and within a five-year span, my mother had four boys—oh boy! It must have been a whirlwind for her, going from being a single professional woman to a mother of four boys within a span of six years. All this activity and energy put my mother to the test.

My mother's name was Elizabeth, and her friends called her Betty, but our family always referred to her as "Bee." Not only was she our mother, but also our coach, trainer, nurse, cook, driver, cheerleader, and psychologist (she loved to quote Lucy from *Charlie Brown*). She was an amazing woman and very protective and supportive of her four boys—a gold-standard role model in nurturing relationships.

My mother was the spiritual leader in our family and held a strong Christian faith. She taught us to pray continuously, and we often prayed together as a family, especially about the challenges we faced. My mother also became involved in the Catholic charismatic renewal, which focused on the totality of the declaration of the gospel, including the importance of a personal relationship with God, along with greater community among believers. She was involved in this spiritual movement throughout the rest of her life. Little did I know at the time that this exposure would be very important for my future relationships.

My mother was in constant prayer for her boys, which set a great example for us. Looking back, it's clear that the woman was a saint. It wasn't too surprising, then, when my 23andMe DNA profile identified my most famous ancestor on my mother's side as Saint Luke the Apostle—who knew we had his DNA?

My mother not only took us to our baseball activities but would also pitch batting practice to us, which became dangerous for her as those line drives were screaming past her head. One time, the ball came back hot, hitting the bridge of her glasses and breaking them in half. She taped them together and continued on, unfazed. As the transportation provider, she drove us around to all our sports activities, and at one time, each of us was on a different team —making it a logistical nightmare. My mother was the key factor for us to get exposure to multiple sports, the arts, religious education, and part-time and summer jobs—influencing our future career choices and interests in indelible ways.

Now, with all this traveling around to sports venues, shopping centers, school, and church, sometimes one of the kids would be left behind or lost. Several times we would get home and realize one of the kids was not there, usually my youngest brother Dave.

My mother was amazingly calm during these times and was very analytical in determining where the missing kid might be. This was before cell phones and digital tracking capabilities, so no technological assistance was available. To her credit, she had a 100% success rate in tracking us down without outside assistance. With four boys to keep track of, my mom developed the ability to thrive under pressure and adapt to almost any circumstance, something we have tried to adopt in our own lives.

Sometimes, in a crisis, you have to carefully weigh your options, even under intense pressure. This is a key part of taking *smart risks*: Think before you leap. One time, my mother took us to a park about ten miles from home for some batting practice. After we unloaded our gear from the car, my mother locked the car doors and put her purse in the trunk for safety. As she was closing the trunk, she didn't realize that her keys were still in there—and thus, the crisis began.

We quickly ran through ways to break into the car, but nothing worked. Given that it was too far to walk, and smartphones had not yet been invented, the only option appeared to be walking to the local gas station to get help. My mother was able to get one of the guys who was filling his car at the gas station to come over to help. After a while, he also failed to get into the car.

My mom was now down to two viable options: Either ask the guy to drive her home and back to get her other set of keys or wait hours until my dad was home and call him from the pay phone to bring her the keys.

She quickly surmised that it was wiser and less painful to get in a car with a total stranger than to wait and call my father. So, she asked, and the stranger agreed to drive her home and back. I stayed with my brothers, not knowing when (or if) my mother would return. After about an hour, she returned and thanked the stranger. She then immediately huddled with me and my brothers and made it clear that not a word of this would be mentioned to my father. It felt like we were making a blood oath of silence, and we never spoke a word about it after that day.

All my mother's investment in sports travel and batting practice started to pay off as we began excelling in baseball, with all of us making All-Star and travel teams. Being the mother of all boys, in a lot of ways, she became "one of the guys." She shared our interests in sports, loved to dress in sweatpants (and rarely wore dresses), enjoyed action movies (especially karate films), and would even take us to professional wrestling matches. She was also ahead of her time and went in and out of the workforce as family demands allowed or required, staying in the workforce in one way or another until her late 70s. She worked not only to earn money but also for the simple joy of engaging with other people.

My mother was never afraid to take risks, but not every risk turns out to be that smart. Once, my mother was invited to a women's luncheon, which required her to step out of her comfort zone and get dressed up. Mom went for it and wore the latest 1960s fashion—a paper dress made to look like the "Yellow

Pages" telephone book. Unfortunately, at the luncheon, the stress on that dress was too great, and it split down the side from top to bottom—a catastrophic wardrobe malfunction. I'm not sure if she wore a dress again until my wedding day.

As the Detroit Public schools became untenable for us to attend, my mother headed back to work as a store cashier to pay for our tuition at the local Catholic school, Precious Blood. The school had a very diverse student body and a disciplined environment with high expectations for student achievement. It was here that I met one of my first mentors, an African American teacher named Mr. Jennings. He had that rare combination of making learning fun while still expecting us to strive to achieve a high standard. He was the kind of teacher who instilled in us an intellectual curiosity and thirst for knowledge of the world around us.

My mother had a strong artistic bent and loved to sing, do arts and crafts, designed banners for her church, and, as a retiree, learned to play the ukulele and perform at senior homes. Maybe in that spirit, she encouraged me to take up playing an instrument, and I chose the trumpet. Talk about getting out of your comfort zone.

I worked hard to master the instrument but made only a little progress. To make it worse, my father hated listening to me practicing in our small house. I don't blame him. Possibly to save her marriage, my mother suggested that maybe the trumpet wasn't for me. Not every smart risk works out; sometimes you learn what you aren't good at, which helps you focus on the things you do well.

My mother was a role model in building relationships with her family, friends, church, community, and in the workplace. She also taught us how to take smart risks and set us up for success through her sacrificial love and support. Although she never attended college, she helped us pursue alignment in our interests and talents and was proud that all four of her sons went on to earn master's degrees or higher, becoming established professionals. She was always encouraging us to get in the game and be players, not just spectators in life, often quite literally. We knew no matter what we had to navigate, no matter how we had to adapt, Bee would be there.

CHAPTER 4
PAPA'S FAMILY TREE

"PAPA WAS A ROLLING STONE" - TEMPTATIONS

Although my father was physically present in the house, he was emotionally distant, focused on work and hobbies, and not fully engaged with his family. He seemed to never fully settle into the role of an attentive husband and father. While my mother was a Polish Tiger mom combined with a living saint, my father was an enigma. He was both complicated and simple at the same time, talented yet self-limiting. He could be charming one day and a stubborn ogre the next. Like most of us, my father's family and upbringing was part of his formation as a person, and understanding my family's history has provided insight into some of his behaviors.

On the day I was born, the artist Norman Rockwell published a famous painting on the cover of the "Saturday Evening

Post." The painting was called the "Family Tree" and showed the lineage of a freckled, red-headed boy. Although the boy looked like a stereotypical "normal American" of that time, the shock generated by the painting originated from the boy's diverse and controversial ancestry. The family tree included everything; from a rancher and saloon girl; to a trapper and his Native American wife; a puritan preacher and a tavern owner, Union and Confederate soldiers; to a pirate patriarch with his Spanish princess bride. When Rockwell was asked why he created this controversial family tree, he said "Everybody had a horse thief or two in his family."

The Crampton family tree was similarly filled with interesting and controversial characters. My father's family first arrived in America four hundred years ago from England, only a generation after the pilgrims landed at Plymouth Rock. The patriarch, Dennis Crampton, took a major risk in search of opportunity and made the journey to the new world landing in Guilford, Connecticut.

My seventh great-grandfather Dennis found himself in trouble with the law from time to time. He was arrested and whipped for slander and horse stealing. Norman Rockwell was explicitly correct in my case; every family has a horse thief—and our family Patriarch started the trend! After a few years, he turned his life around and eventually became a prosperous landowner.

The Crampton family has been around for the development of the country from its earliest days. Members of the family served in the military, including all the major wars since the Revolution. The family developed some unique traditions that have carried on for generations. For example, my oldest son Nathan is named after his grandfather, who was named after his grandfather. There has been a Nathan/Nathaniel Crampton in at least every other generation going back over two hundred years. Recently, my son Nathan honored me by naming his son Kevin. Hopefully, the Nathan and Kevin streak will continue in future generations.

With the opening of the Erie Canal, my branch of the family tree made the journey by water to what had been called the Northwest Territories (think more Northwestern University in Chicago and less Washington state) and eventually settled in Michigan. It was at this time the family appeared to drop the letter "p" from Crampton, resulting in the much more economical Cramton. The clan established themselves around the farming community of Saint Charles in mid-Michigan over one hundred miles northwest of Detroit.

Continuing the family's tradition of service, several Michigan Cramtons served the Union in the Civil War. One of my cousins, Louis Cramton, served several decades in Congress, representing the family's mid-Michigan district. Given that his father fought in the Civil War, and he was from the party of Lincoln, Louis developed a strong interest in historically Black colleges and was instrumental in securing funding for Howard University in Washington D.C., where the Cramton Auditorium is named in his honor. His brother, Fred Cramton, headed from Michigan down to Montgomery, Alabama, after the Civil War to start a lumber business, becoming a very successful businessman and the leader and key financial backer behind the building of the Cramton Bowl, which would go on to host the likes of the Alabama Crimson Tide, Auburn Tigers, Babe Ruth and Lou Gehrig, negro league baseball, and Alabama State football games.

Like the Rockwell painting, my father's family tree was varied and multi-branched. His lineage was filled with innovators and risk takers, from lumber business magnates to Hollywood actors and even a family of trapeze artists—the Flying Melzoras.

My Aunt Jane and her family of aerial trapeze artists, the "Flying Melzoras," were performers with the "Greatest Show on Earth," the Ringling Brothers and Barnum & Bailey Circus. My aunt, who performed with her family until she was sixty-four years old, was the catcher, who swung upside down by her legs on the trapeze, catching the flyer, who is leaping through the air from another trapeze, a role that eventually saw her inducted, along with her family, into the Circus Hall of Fame. Her sons would go on to pioneer various trapeze and other circus performances as they followed in her flying footsteps.

The Flying Melzoras were a family that exemplified the key attributes required to pursue the Dream, building strong relational capital and trust within the family to take on the trapeze, turning what would be unacceptably risky behavior to everyone else into smart, calculated risks, pursuing a career that matched their skills and interests, and entertaining thousands in the crowd of spectators as key Circus Center Ring players.

As the Flying Melzoras were soaring in the "Greatest Show on Earth," my cousin Arthur Lake was becoming very famous as the character Dagwood Bumstead, starring in twenty-eight Hollywood-produced "Blondie" movies, the series of movies based on the comic strip created by Chic Young. At a young age, Arthur and his sister Florence began working in show business, where he made his screen acting debut at the age of five in the silent film "Jack and the Beanstalk." Florence became a successful actress in comedy films and was cast in the long-running TV series "Lassie," while Arthur signed with Universal Pictures and played in multiple westerns and comedy roles. He eventually moved on to RKO Radio Pictures, where he played in several movies, including the classic film, "Topper," but it was his twelve-year stint as "Dagwood" in "Blondie," both on radio and in films, that earned Lake his star on the Hollywood Walk of Fame.

The family was very proud of Arthur and his incredible success, but what wasn't talked about was the family situation surrounding his wife, Patricia. She grew up in San Simeon, California at Hearst Castle, where the open secret was that Patricia was the daughter of newspaper magnate William Randolf Hearst and his long-term mistress, film star Marion Davies. The Lakes were married at Hearst Castle and William Randolph Hearst walked Patricia down the aisle. Talk about a colorful family history.

In the early twentieth century, Nathan Cramton moved his family to join the flood of people relocating to Detroit. At the time, the city was experiencing a "gold rush" created by the automobile revolution and the many opportunities it afforded. Detroit was making the transition from another Midwest regional city into the motor capital of the world—Motown.

While many of the newcomers, like my mother's family, were working in the auto plants of Ford, GM, and Chrysler, my father's family focused on the construction business, building the factories and infrastructure to support the growth in the auto industry.

The pay for this was much better than the farming community the family came from, but there were a few unforeseen consequences that came with this new line of work. This included weather-dependent working availability (which made rain, snow, and very cold weather unpaid days off), and the jobs were project-specific (ending when the project was complete). These factors made household income variable and unpredictable, requiring strong financial discipline and a rainy-day fund to survive. Furthermore, the construction industry had a hard-living, hard-drinking culture that was not very conducive to family life.

My great-grandfather, Nathan, moved his family into a rental house in Detroit and started work in the construction business, later joined by his sons, including my grandfather, Montello (Monty for short). Monty married relatively young and had two children, Francis and Kenneth. Unfortunately, his marriage ended in divorce when the kids were young, and my grandfather ended up with full custody. Given he was incapable of taking care of the kids alone, he relied on my great-grandmother and extended family to raise them. Due to the demands of his work and keeping the family afloat, my grandfather never developed close and nurturing relationships with his children.

A few years later, my grandfather married my grandmother, Mary, who was eleven years his junior and in a hurry to get out of her father's house. My grandmother suffered a tragedy as a young girl when her mother died during the Spanish Flu pandemic, which killed around fifty million people worldwide. Her father remarried, and the relationship with her stepmother was strained at best.

Mary grew up Catholic, but because she was marrying a divorcee, she could not get married in the church. Given my grandfather grew up with no church affiliation and my grandmother abandoned her childhood faith, my father grew up in an environment devoid of spiritual practice and formation.

My father, Nathan (or Nick), and his sister Betty were born during the Great Depression and grew up in that difficult economic environment as well as the turmoil caused by World War II. The depression was devastating to Detroit, and finding work became almost impossible. My great-grandfather defaulted on his mortgage and was forced into government housing and food assistance, including receiving a block of free cheese each week.

The little work Monty managed to find was used to pay for cigarettes, alcohol, and gambling—with his favorite being playing the ponies at the racetrack. He would often disappear after receiving his paycheck on Friday, quickly cashing in his check and heading to the bar to gamble and drink it away. My grandmother finally got wise to his habits and would go to his favorite bar on Friday. She waited for him to arrive so she could demand enough money for family expenses before their income completely disappeared.

My father developed his love for athletics during these hard times, becoming a star athlete playing on two state champion runner-up baseball teams when baseball was truly the American pastime. He also played basketball and was a Golden Gloves boxer. Although he never showed much interest in coaching his four sons, from time to time he would come on the backyard court to demonstrate his set shot and show us how to do a proper lay-up.

He had a spectator's interest in all major sports, but boxing seemed to have a special place, given his previous success. We would find him sparing in the air with his huge forearms, reliving some glorious previous match. Through my father's love of boxing, my brothers and I connected with George Foreman at a chance encounter. We were shocked to discover he was familiar with one of the old boxing gyms my father frequented. This engaged conversation around the Kronk gym became the point of connection we had with the two-time heavyweight champion.

Although my grandfather was not engaged much with his family, my father idolized him and followed in his footsteps. This included leaving high school early to get into the reinforced steel construction business. They worked on most jobs together and became drinking buddies, often going to the racetrack to bet on the ponies.

Nick's lifestyle changed drastically when he was drafted into the Army. His time in the service influenced him into developing a more disciplined and hardline approach to both his job and family.

At home, my father liked to use terms from his military service like "KP (Kitchen Patrol) duty" when he wanted us to clean up or help in food prep. He must have had a lot of experience doing KP since he was the master at preparing mashed potatoes for family holiday meals. For the weekend, he would tell us we were getting up early for a "GI Party" to clean up our rooms. He would threaten to toss a quarter on our beds, anticipating a sharp bounce to indicate we had made them correctly.

Although the four of us boys were mostly well-behaved, our high "activity" level limited my parents' friend group to a very small few who could keep up. My cousins were one of those exceptions, and it was nearly apocalyptic when we got together with my cousins, the Urams. Like our family, the Urams had four boys, but they broke the mold by having an additional baby girl. The Urams lived in the old Polish neighborhood my mother grew up in until they later moved to a semi-rural area over fifty miles south of Motown. We would rotate visiting each other's homes on holidays and get together for special events like summer picnics.

One thing I quickly learned is that our two families functioned in different time zones. There was Cramton time, which was always ahead of eastern standard time, stemming from my father's desire to always be early. Uram time, on the other hand, always ran an hour or more late. When the Urams were coming our way, we set up a betting line going as to when they would show up. After a while, my mother would tell them the start time was an hour earlier, a mostly successful strategy to avoid conflict.

We had a blast together, and the fun of visiting with our extended family could lead to some over-exuberance. One time my father felt compelled to dial us down and teach us a lesson. At the time, all of us boys were sleeping in one bedroom with two sets of bunk beds. Our cousins came over for Christmas and broke both our new toys and our beds. In response, my father required us to sleep with our mattresses on the floor for a few months. Given our neighborhood had a rat problem, I was always listening for sounds at night.

Clearly, my father's approach to discipline was tough, but upon reflection, in his own way he was providing a foundation that would help me manage the challenging people and situations faced throughout my life.

His old-school philosophy dictated that he was the breadwinner, and my mother was the homemaker running the family. Outside of working to provide, he saw few obligations to his family and tended to engage in his hobbies—primarily gambling on horses and drinking with his friends. Although he was in the house, he wasn't truly present in most family interactions, preferring TV to dialogue. He thought that providing economically was his part of the deal but missed developing relationships with his spouse and children.

Although my father was disciplined and a hard worker, when he was presented with greater responsibilities and the chance to advance in his career, he chose not to pursue them due to a fear of failure. My father had multiple positive characteristics that could have resulted in significant success, but he was deeply self-limiting and adopted behaviors like drinking and gambling that ate away at his talents.

One of my earliest memories was learning to play cards with my aunt and grandparents, including penny poker. I became very good. I learned how to read the racing form and would go to the track from time to time. I quickly noticed we only talked about the winning races and were quiet about the losers, but the losing tickets remained littered all over the track floor no matter how much we tried to ignore them.

Instead of investing in developing themselves through education or training, my family would sit around and fantasize for hours about winning the lottery or hitting the trifecta at the races. This struck me as pointless, so I took a different path, committed to investing in myself and avoiding those destructive vices. I attempted to surround myself with the right personal, professional, and spiritual relationships to help stay on track.

To be fair to my father, the demands of work and the financial responsibilities of family can easily blind you to the more important relational and communal aspects of life. Those moments with our families are fleeting and precious, but this can be difficult to see when you're constantly bogged down with worry. Although I have made progress in these areas, I've often come up short when I allowed my work to get in the way of family engagement. My wife has been a good accountability partner alerting me when my priorities were wrong.

My father did redeem himself as a grandfather, as that's where he excelled. Perhaps he concluded that he missed so much with his own kids that he wouldn't forfeit his second chance.

PART 2
SHIFTING GEARS

The next three chapters explore key early transitions of moving, college, early professional experiences, and finding your life partner. Many of my experiences in Motown helped prepare me to navigate these transitions. A well-tuned life means adapting to the constant changes you will face, especially during times of transition.

CHAPTER 5
MEETING THE REDHEAD

"YOU ARE THE SUNSHINE OF MY LIFE" - STEVIE WONDER

Although by the time I started high school Detroit was getting more dangerous because of drugs and violent crime in our neighborhood, it was the death of my grandfather, and my father's subsequent mourning of him, that prompted us to consider moving out of the city. About a year after my grandfather's passing, my grandmother and aunt decided they wanted to move to the suburbs. This triggered my mother's all-out search for a house.

My parents had little savings for a down payment, an income history that was up and down, and because they always rented, had built no home equity, leaving them with limited options. To maximize what we could afford, while minimizing the down-payment requirements, our realtor concluded that a loan through the Veterans Administration (VA), leveraging my father's military service, would be the best strategy. Unfortunately, because of the longer governmental approval process, most sellers did not want the hassle of a buyers' VA loan.

My mother did extensive research on neighborhoods and homes in our price range, looking for sellers who would be flexible on financing, and praying constantly, something we all participated in. It seemed like we walked through over thirty houses in the western suburbs of Detroit. There were several near misses, and we were getting discouraged that we wouldn't be able to find the right place. But then, through what seemed like divine intervention, we found a house in Garden City, about fifteen miles southwest of where we were living. It had everything we needed, and even a family room with a fireplace, plus the seller was willing to accept all of our terms. For us, it was nothing short of a miracle.

We moved before the start of my junior year, which was a tough time to make that kind of transition. I had been attending the all-boys Catholic Central High School, one of the top schools in the city and just a few blocks from my old house in Detroit. Given that my parents had committed all their financial resources to buying this new house, they were not in a position to continue to fund my Catholic school education.

That fall, my brothers and I started in the Garden City public schools. Moving to a new school at this stage was difficult for me, and I missed my friends and teachers. We had moved late in the summer, and I had not yet developed any friendships, so the new school was very lonely for me. After the first month, I told my mother I was unhappy, and reminded her that my oldest cousin was allowed to finish out high school when his family had moved fifty miles away.

My mother responded that if we could figure out a way to solve the funding issue and manage the commute, I could finish up at Catholic Central. She contacted the principal and appealed to him, negotiating a 50% tuition discount if I agreed to come in early several mornings a week to do set-up. To fund the other 50%, I needed to get a job. I found a position as a bagger and parking lot cart collector at the local grocery store, which, along with my share of the family paper route, provided enough money to pay the rest of my tuition.

The next hurdle was making the fifteen-mile commute each way. Although we had a second car, I did not initially have my license and it would have been a significant burden for my mother to commit to driving back and forth every day. In the end, we developed a combination transportation plan, including her driving me a few days, and other days driving to a pick-up point to get in a carpool. The last resort was taking the public bus, which had a bus stop half a mile from the school and ended a few miles from my new home.

So, my mother and I were able to pull this off, and I returned to Catholic Central for the second half of my junior year. We worked hard to make it work, but I was about to learn to "be careful what you wish for." Sometimes God has other plans.

While it was good to be back in a familiar environment with my friends, the costs of being there were extremely high. Instead of being a few blocks away from school, the fifteen-mile daily commute each way could be exhausting. It effectively eliminated my ability to play sports or participate in after-school activities. I was also constantly working before and after school and on weekends to pay the tuition. Life had become joyless, and I began to question my decision.

As the semester was ending, I was seriously reevaluating my decision. One of the things I really missed was playing sports. At the same time, my brothers were fighting through their first-year transition and were starting to develop friendships and get acclimated to our new community.

During the year, I was going through driver's education to get my license, which is a rite of passage in the Motor City. For some reason, my mother would take me to the family cemetery to practice; maybe it was a warning about smart risks. She also gave us some money to buy an above-ground pool kit for the backyard. My brothers and I dug out the site with shovels to get it deep enough to dive in and constructed the pool without adult supervision. For diving platforms, we found discarded pallets from the local grocery store that we painted and attached to the pool at each end. All of us, especially my brother, Mark, who earned the aquatic nickname "Sharky," enjoyed the fruits of our labor by spending plenty of time in the pool.

During that summer, a fateful opportunity came up. Mark, who was eighteen months younger than me, had played on the junior high basketball team and was entering high school. He mentioned that the high school was offering a summer basketball program, and I should join him—so I did. For the first time in months, I was having fun and developing new friendships.

The basketball team the previous year was ranked as one of the best Class A teams in the state, but all the starters and key subs had graduated, leaving only one incoming senior, a few juniors, and a bunch of young but promising new high schoolers, including Mark. Given the youth and inexperience of the team, I figured I could probably break into the starting lineup. Along with the new relationships I was developing, the opportunity to play basketball with my brother helped push me to get into the transfer portal and risk finishing out my high school career in Garden City.

As fate would have it, early in the new school year, I had my first encounter with the Redhead. My brother and I were early for our zero-hour study hall and the school was having student elections. Given we were two tall guys who literally stood out in the lunchroom, a striking redhead, who herself was over 5' 8", came over and introduced herself as Faye Morris. With her red hair and blue eyes, she was the rarest combination in the world (less than 0.02% of the population). Faye asked if she could assist us in voting. Although we knew none of the candidates, we went ahead and voted, with Faye telling us what she thought were the best choices. Little did I know at the time that this was the start of something special. Years later, in another very important political event, Mark would win "sexiest man" in his mock senior class elections.

After that first meeting, I would often see Faye during our zero-hour study hall. On game day for the girls' basketball team, Faye would wear her team t-shirt, and we would chat about who she was playing and make small talk. A few weeks later, we had the conversation that launched everything. She had been elected to the homecoming court and needed a date. She had broken up with her previous boyfriend and wasn't too interested in other suitors. She was under pressure from the student advisor to get a date; if she didn't, the advisor would select one for her, making her desperate to act.

Avoiding an assigned date gave her the courage that fateful morning to ask me if I would be her date and escort her onto the field for the homecoming ceremony, and to the dance. I froze; I had not seen this coming. I replied, "Can I think about it and get back to you?" She must have been mortified but said "Sure." As I was processing the request, I asked  my friends what they thought, and they all said Faye was very nice and that I should help her out. That evening, I discussed it with my mother, and she said that this girl must be desperate, and I should be a good Samaritan and do it.

The next morning, to her relief, I told her I would be her date. A few days later, the homecoming festivities were on, and I was dressed up in a suit escorting her onto the football field with hundreds of people in the stands looking at us. It was all a bit surreal. Faye's father had passed away a few years earlier, so her brother Tim joined us on the field. Given the whirlwind nature of the whole thing, her mother invited me over to their house after the football game to get to know them. The next evening was dinner and the homecoming dance. We had a good time and seemed to hit it off; there was something there.

As we talked, we found several common interests, including sports and history. On the other hand, it was clear that we came from very different cultural backgrounds, with me growing up in Detroit and being a Catholic and her being a suburban Baptist gal. My Detroit upbringing clearly made me a bit rough around the edges. Even things like the vegetables we ate were different;

she liked fresh, and I only knew canned. She ate slowly and liked to have conversations during meals. I ate fast, with limited conversation, maybe because I had three brothers who would take seconds if I hesitated. Likewise, growing up in Detroit with all boys resulted in me using some salty language and "urban phases" that lasted until I was later gentrified.

As we began dating, it didn't take long to figure out that she was an absolute gem. Faye was the rarest combination in the world, not just physically, but in all the other ways. While I knew early that she was the girl for me, she took her time. In fact, it was her mother who could see I was a "diamond in the rough" much sooner than Faye did.

When you are looking for a life partner, along with being attracted to each other, enjoying their personality, and having some common interests, it's important to have a common spiritual focus. Again, I grew up Catholic and the Redhead was very much a Baptist. Faye's mother went to Wheaton College with Evangelist Billy Graham, who officiated her wedding to Faye's father, and her grandmother Faye, for whom she was named, was Graham's first church secretary. Although the Redhead and I came from different faith backgrounds, we had both been exposed to the evangelical Christian movement at the time, which focused on a deeper, personal relationship with God. Faye's evangelical religious experience was like scenes from the movie *The Jesus Revolution*. This ended up being a key anchor in our relationship, and one in which she was a fabulous role model, both then and now. She was instrumental in helping me to make a deeper commitment to my faith and has been a great spiritual mentor ever since.

As our senior year rolled on, we spent more time together, and I fell deeper in love with the Redhead. I was so certain she was the one for me that I had a t-shirt made in our school colors that said "Faye Cramton." I didn't give it to her at the time, not wanting to jump the gun, but the intent in my heart and mind was clear. I was all in on building something with Faye that would last.

When the boys' hoops season began, the team struggled because of our inexperience and youth, but I was getting better and better as the season went on. During an away game in February, everything came together. They say everyone gets their fifteen minutes of fame, and mine happened that night. Before the three-point shot and with no shot clock in high school, I scored thirty-five points in the game. This was so rare in Class A basketball that I made headlines in the local newspapers, and on that night, it appeared that I was the leading scorer in the state of Michigan—which had a half-dozen future NBA players on high school teams at the time.

Although this was a great accomplishment, it was the next home game a few days later that produced a legendary moment. As with all home games, the home team players are usually announced to some cheers or applause from friends and parents. But that night, the announcer, Steve McGowan, a high school student and friend of mine, was introducing the starters, and I was going to be the last one. As I was getting ready to run out onto the court, I was shocked to hear the words "Starting at forward, at 6' 4", Kevin "Doctor K" Cramton"! I ran out and looked at the announcer, and at my coach, who was red in the face. I was no Julius Erving, but the "Doctor J"—inspired name stuck. I never lived it down, especially since my coach made sure in no uncertain terms that "Doctor K" announcements were a one-and-done event.

You would think, decades later, that this "Doctor K" story would be forgotten—but no, my three brothers, who were coaches and PE teachers, loved bringing it up. A few years ago, on one of our common text exchanges, we were talking about gym shoes, and Mark said he wanted some 70s "Doctor K" Converse High Tops. I decided to take it to the next level and design my own custom "Doctor K" 70s Converses. On top of that, my daughter, Rose, made me a "Breaking Ankles from 1977" logo to go with my sweet black leather high-top Converse All-Stars. This shoe line has obviously been in high demand, worn by people around the world. The key is to have a pair signed by "Doctor K" himself, you know, for resale value.

As my high school basketball season was winding down, I continued to have some success, with several double-doubles in points and rebounds. Although I improved a lot over the season, I was not under any illusion that, as a 6'4" forward, I had the potential to play at the major college level. After the season ended, I got a few postseason honors and began to focus on school and my upcoming college decision. Most of the things we focus on in life come and go, but it's how they form us that carries forward.

With a solid foundation from previous semesters, I focused on several of the more challenging writing, political science, economics, and accounting classes. A couple of my favorite teachers were Ms. Brammer, who made political science fun and was very encouraging about my future college pursuits, and Mr. Lee, who exposed me to the language of business in accounting and finance.

For my project in media class, I teamed up with my high school announcer friend Steve, my brother, and a neighborhood friend to produce our version of the CBS "Slam Dunk Competition" TV show, filmed using the garage hoop in the driveway. Decades later, we pulled this film out of the archives and were amazed at how young, thin, and athletic we looked, especially in those 70s-style short-shorts. Using modern technology, we were able to edit it into an updated parody.

In the spring, I decided to try something new and went out for track and field. Although I ran the 220 and 440 (back when it was in yards, not meters), I focused on the high jump. Given that I had no experience with the high jump, I spent most of my time working on the "Fosbury Flop" technique. Like most new things, it was initially awkward, but I stuck with it. By the end of the season, I had made some progress and won the city track and field meet in the high jump—my first and only gold medal.

As the time for my college decision approached, I was focused on some of the best universities in the Midwest, including Notre Dame, the University of Michigan, and Michigan State. These were all relatively close to home, came with a great college atmosphere, and would position me well for a future career. They were all excellent schools, but once the Redhead decided that she was going to be a Spartan, I quickly decided to follow suit.

Looking back on it, my senior year in high school was the most enjoyable and impactful period in my life. It all came together in a totally unexpected way. *My* plan had been to finish up at my old high school, but it seemed like my steps were divinely guided in another direction. During that amazing year, I found my future life partner, took several smart risks that actually worked out, tried new things, and got some exposure to potential future career paths. I was an active player, participating and engaged in the world around me. I learned that year what Proverbs 16:9 says, "The mind of man plans his way, But the Lord directs his steps." (NASB) As Faye and I walked forward, I knew that a great adventure was just beginning.

CHAPTER 6
GOING OFF TO COLLEGE

"LET'S GET IT ON" - MARVIN GAYE

I was the first person in my immediate family to go to college. My father, who left high school early to work for my grandfather, didn't know what to think of higher education. He expected me to join the family vocation in construction, but my mother was supportive of my pursuits. My family didn't have anything like a college fund for me or my siblings, so it was up to us to raise the money to pay for our education. When my parents dropped me off at Michigan State, my father gave me a twenty-dollar bill—the only direct financial assistance I would receive. Through working both summers and during the school year, I was able to self-fund my undergraduate education without taking out student loans.

My first summer job was in the moving business. After some searching, I came across the local agent of a national moving company who needed help. The work was physically demanding but paid well, however I quickly noticed that a combination of that physically demanding labor, along with a culture of smoking and drinking alcohol, took a major toll on the longer-tenured employees. This ended up being good motivation for me to do well in school.

During my second summer in the moving business, my boss thought I had some potential, and I was trained as a packer. This was an important and more highly valued job, and I was responsible for carefully wrapping and boxing household goods for the move. I spent most of my last two years as a lead packer, functioning as the key customer interface for this stage of the moving process. I would bring in my own crew if needed, which in many cases were my brothers, and my compensation was paid on a per-box basis, incentivizing efficiency. My youngest brothers would work for me as the muscle, moving boxes around and doing jobs no one else wanted. On one occasion, the driver leading the move asked my younger brothers to go pick up some beer. After a few moments of silence, my brother asked if the driver knew he was only sixteen, and that plan was quickly aborted.

I became quite good at running the packing operation, giving me my first taste of running a business. The elements of success were all present for me: Relationship building with clients and my team, taking risks to pursue an entrepreneurial opportunity and stepping up when it came to engaging as a leader.

Speaking of being engaged with the world around you, my first college roommate was a Hawaiian, Kimo Kippen, who came to Michigan State with an interest in the veterinarian program. I had never roomed with anyone outside of my siblings, and despite our differences, he was very personable, and we got along well. It was interesting to see him in his first Michigan winter experience, something I had grown accustomed to over the years. After the first snow, he was outside making snow angels and building snowmen. I admired his ability to adapt to new surroundings and how he connected with new people; this firsthand example taught me the importance of choosing to act, to get "into the game."

Life at college was the first time I was away from home for an extended period of time, but the transition was easier because the Redhead was there. One of our favorite dates was the "Burger King Special" on Sundays. The dorms were closed, and we would spend quality time together enjoying one-dollar whoppers and interesting conversation.

Faye and I decided to get involved in the local community by taking jobs in the inner-city after-school programs in Lansing. I ran the after-school basketball programs and Faye did ballet, gymnastics, and cooking classes. Faye developed a passion for working with children that would later develop into a career in elementary education. My work reminded me of my childhood in Motown playing hoops with the neighborhood kids. My students were especially surprised when I threw down a few dunks.

We became active participants in a campus Christian group linked to the Assemblies of God. The group was led by Ren Wallen, who had a great way of relating to young people. Having a spiritual anchor on campus was a great benefit as we matured, and the group provided a meeting place that led to several long-lasting friendships. Our time in the group also offered a bridge between our religious backgrounds, something resembling a mixture of my charismatic Catholic upbringing and Faye's evangelical "Jesus Movement" experiences.

At the end of my second year, I was accepted into the business school—the culmination of a multi-year process of discovering my vocational calling. At the same time, I was able to satisfy my interest in coaching and teaching through after-school and volunteer work. In my experience, this balance between what you're good at and what you love is essential for a healthy life.

After three years of dating, Faye and I were engaged during the Christmas break of that year. She wanted a certain style ring and wasn't convinced I could manage to find the exact one she wanted, so we shopped for it together. The ring we found had a ruby within an old-fashioned filigree design—a perfect fit for my Redhead. After we got the ring from the jewelers, we had a somewhat anticlimactic ring ceremony in the parking lot. For a number of practical and financial reasons, we decided to set the wedding date for when I graduated two years later.

As we finished our undergraduate degrees, we began undertaking several important career decisions. The Redhead had an opportunity for an elementary school paid internship, but it would extend her graduation date by one year. At the same time, I was evaluating graduating and beginning my career versus pursuing a master's degree in business. Given that the job market was not the best at the time, I took a serious look at going to graduate school. After getting accepted to the MBA program, we found a way to make the tuition affordable through a combination of scholarship money and a graduate assistantship. This would enable me to go to graduate school while Faye was working and finishing her degree.

A short time after graduating with a degree in Business Administration, the Redhead and I were getting married, after five years of dating. The wedding was unique and very ecumenical. The event was hosted at the Baptist Church the Redhead grew up in, while our Assembly of God campus pastor officiated the ceremony, and my mother's charismatic Catholic parish priest, along with Faye's Baptist minister, were on the platform with us. With all those clergy present, we felt like we were clearly married in the presence of God.

We had little money, so the reception was a lovely but simple event at the church hall. Our "chariot" leaving the event was my eleven-year-old blue and rusted Chevy Nova decked out for the wedding. Our first night together was at the Knight's Inn, a local motel, and we were both exhausted from the events of the day. The honeymoon would have to wait since Faye had summer classes and I was starting my graduate assistantship. We settled into married housing at University Village and started our new life together.

For my graduate assistantship, I was selected to be an undergraduate academic advisor for the business school. This would become one of the most formative experiences of my life. The role required personal relationship building, public speaking, familiarity with program offerings, the ability to match skills with interests, and plenty of coaching. The public speaking component required talking to large parent-student orientation groups. This taught me how to craft an effective presentation, the importance of reading the audience, and how to respond in an extemporaneous way to connect with my listeners.

My role also included one-on-one counseling for students who were making career and life decisions. I took this responsibility seriously and became proficient at helping the students walk through their decision processes, including delineating key pros and cons. This meant performing a realistic assessment of how the student's skills and capabilities best aligned with programs offered by the business school or potential majors in other areas. This advisory role was foundational to how I would live my life and was one of my key motivations for writing this book.

Along with new experiences and challenges, graduate school provided some of my first professional leadership experiences. At the encouragement of our program advisor, Joel Shulman, I was elected the president of the finance club, which was one of the key business school organizations. We had monthly professional business speakers, a trip to the Chicago Mercantile Exchange, and an annual banquet with a big-name speaker that I needed to organize and manage. Joel and I have been friends ever since, including my having the privilege to hold up one of the legs of his chair at my first Jewish wedding. We could not have imagined at the time that several decades later I would be on the platform with Joel ringing the opening bell at the NASDAQ stock exchange on live TV with a large multi-story projection in Times Square.

The relationships, leadership opportunities, and skills I built during this time were indispensable for the next stage of my life and career.

CHAPTER 7
JOINING CORPORATE AMERICA

"AIN'T NOTHING LIKE THE REAL THING" - MARVIN GAYE

It was time to enter the real world of professional careers and family life, and I was grateful to have the Redhead by my side. As graduation from the MBA program approached, the job market was significantly better than two years previous, large employers were interested in students with MBA degrees, and my recent university leadership roles were valuable and had provided me with good networking introductions. I had several interviews and ended up with five job offers, one in banking, two with Big Three auto companies, and two with large computer companies. Although I had grown up in Motown and the auto business, the two computer companies were very attractive, given that the information revolution was still in its early stages and promised a bright future.

After a lot of analysis, and in consultation and prayer with the Redhead, I accepted a position in the computer industry at Detroit-based Burroughs Corporation. The combination of the industry, my interest in the specific job opportunity, and the ability to stay close to home were key factors in our decision. The company had a long history as a pioneer in the adding-machine business, starting with mechanical and then transitioning to one of the country's largest producers of mainframe computers. During World War II, Burroughs was part of Detroit's Arsenal of Democracy, building the Norden bombsight, while Ford was building bombers on an assembly line a few miles away.

I started in the corporate treasury office in midtown Detroit, less than a mile from the original Motown Music studio and headquarters. Burroughs had a rotational development program, so I had several different treasury assignments. It was during one of these rotational assignments that I met my first career mentor, Phil Schultz. After his undergraduate education and a stint in Vietnam as a helicopter gunship pilot, he went on to an MBA at USC, where he would become a big Trojan football fan. He was great at providing constructive feedback and career counseling. I would seek his advice throughout my career, and he was always generous with his time. Over the years, we enjoyed reconnecting in Los Angeles for a USC game at the Coliseum.

Faye and I moved into a nice apartment in Springwells Park in Dearborn, Michigan. These apartments and townhouses were originally built by Ford to house members of its management team, given the proximity to its headquarters and the world's largest industrial complex at the Rouge. Our adjacent neighbors included a Polish auto retiree who reminded me of my mother's uncles, and Bruce, an African American guy about our age who worked in Purchasing for Chrysler. Because of our shared love of basketball, R&B, and sports cars, Bruce and I hit it off. In fact, it's because of Bruce that I saw the "Bad Boy" Pistons win two NBA championships.

At the time, Burroughs was run by Michael Blumenthal, the former Treasury Secretary and a seasoned CEO. We had a good supply of small-denomination US currency in the vault, which had his signature on it, that would be given out to selected visitors.

After a few years, I moved to an assignment in corporate finance that would significantly impact my future career. It was at this time that Burroughs decided to lead the first major computer industry consolidation move with the acquisition of Sperry Corporation, one of the iconic pioneers in computing. Given that Sperry was about the same size as Burroughs, this was, at that time, the largest computer industry deal ever. The deal's successful execution came down to our ability to finance it. My full-time job involved assisting the Corporate Treasurer in analyzing and executing the financing package. This meant I got to go to meetings with the CEO, worked with Wall Street and bankers to finance the deal, and had a front-row seat on how these kinds of deals are done from start to finish. The transaction demonstrated the importance of relationships, assessing risks, looking at an array of different structures, and actively managing the process. It was during this time I met Fares Noujaim, who was working at Goldman Sachs early in his career. Given we were both junior guys at the time, we ended up building a friendship that has lasted decades. Fares's is a great immigrant success story, as his family is from Lebanon, and he has worked his way to the top echelons of global finance.

After the deal was done, I received a company achievement award in recognition of my efforts. Shortly after this, the integration and transition planning commenced, and the combined company, renamed Unisys, decided to put its headquarters in Philadelphia where Sperry was located.

During this same period, my wife and I purchased our first house and had our first child, Nathan. This was an exciting time and began the family-raising stage of our lives. Parenting is a whole new learning experience but requires the same four keys to successful navigation as the rest of life— which is easier said than done.

We followed a Cramton family tradition and named him after his grandfather Nathan and his middle name, Frederick, after Faye's father. From an early age, Nathan was immersed in Motown music. We have him on video at a young age singing out his favorite Motown song, and he would eventually become a lead singer in a high school rock band before moving on to other entertainment endeavors.

With the Company moving to Philly, we had some key decisions to make regarding career and family. Faye and I took an exploratory trip to Philly to look at the area and potential houses. One thing became clear: We could not afford the same kind of house on the East Coast and would have to live with something less than what we had in Michigan. At the same time, I began to reach out to my network to see if there were other opportunities.

A friend of mine at Ford, Ken Behr, told me about an opportunity in Treasury at Ford Credit. My experience at Burroughs was a great fit for what they were looking for. Given Ford Credit was the world's third largest corporate borrower at the time, after GE Capital and GMAC, they liked all the financings I had worked on to fund the Sperry deal. Furthermore, I had already had several relationships with the investment and commercial banks Ford worked with.

As I compared the two opportunities, the family advantages were a key factor. Ford had a great reputation for its management development, offering opportunities to work in various areas of the company. We decided to accept the Ford Credit offer, beginning a long and eventful two decades with the company.

At Ford Credit, I had the opportunity to work with Wall Street to raise the billions in funding required to finance auto loans and leases. It offered me the opportunity to spend a lot of time in New York. With the Bloomberg terminals on my desk, I was in the market daily, working with the investment bankers to raise funding to meet our business needs.

At the time, Ford was trying to grow its financial services business. With my merger and acquisition (M&A) experience from Burroughs, I was asked to join the team on an acquisition of a large leasing company—my first M&A experience for Ford. This ended up being a foreshadowing of future M&A deals I would work on later in my career.

Ford encouraged a wide range of experiences across the global enterprise, with roles in automotive components (a vestige of Henry Ford I and his early vertically integrated business strategy), including the electronics and climate-control divisions. This experience was invaluable when I later ran several automotive component businesses.

During my tenure in the automotive components group, I was asked to work on a special M&A project for the head of finance. This was an acquisition of a company in the newly independent country of Czechoslovakia right after the fall of the Soviet Union. This was a surreal experience, as I flew into the Prague city airport, which still had anti-aircraft guns in their seemingly *Casablanca*-inspired rainy, dimly lit airport. We cleared customs, were met by our escorts, and headed for our next flight to Ostrava, the headquarters of the company we were considering acquiring. We got on a relatively small airplane, where we had to shift around seats to balance the weight. The seats were made of mesh and the cabin service was a warm can of Coke. To say I was a bit nervous was an understatement. I tried to get some sleep and attempted not to think about my uncomfortable seat. As we were approaching Ostrava, we circled the airport, and you could see all the anti-aircraft guns near the landing strip. I was girding my body for the landing, and then, to my surprise, we came down as smooth as silk and taxied to a stop. As we were disembarking the aircraft, I mentioned to the flight attendant how smooth the landing was. She responded that it should have been, since the man flying our little commercial passenger plane had been one of the top Czech military pilots, flying MIG jets just weeks before.

We had dinner and were briefed that night, then headed out the next morning to the main manufacturing facilities. We learned that the Company had about 5,000 employees that were mostly women, given that it was lighter manufacturing. This plant had been a center of excellence in the Soviet bloc for these products for years. Within the Soviet system, there was limited geographic mobility, and only a few places to work. So, if you were a woman, this was one of your few choices, whereas the men were channeled to the local steel plants.

We were told that we were in competition with a prominent German auto supplier for the Company. The Germans had been very active acquiring Czech companies, including VW's purchase of Skoda. As we drove into the facilities in our caravan of Ford vehicles, we were shocked to see the entranceway lined with employees waving the American Flag. It quickly became clear that the Czech employees favored the Americans over the Germans, which wasn't too surprising given their memories of WWII and the recent well-publicized economic Blitzkrieg of German acquisitions. We were welcomed like liberating World War II GIs, and before touring the facilities, we were fed a large meat-and-potatoes lunch. It felt like something my Polish grandmother would make.

The facilities and engineering capabilities were relatively good. Although it had too many people, the government was providing employment incentives. The only key sticking point was the potential environmental issues, for which we needed an ironclad indemnity. Once that issue was resolved and the government incentive package agreed to, the transaction moved relatively quickly to completion. This ended up being both a great learning experience and one of my most fascinating career transactions, with an array of unexpected twists and turns.

During my time in Eastern Europe, I ended up with a lingering illness that resulted in constant fatigue and flu-like symptoms that weren't getting better. After a series of tests and a lot of prayer, the doctors determined that I had post-viral syndrome, in which my body was still fighting a prior viral infection. This challenging up-and-down six-month period was one of those times when I heavily relied on my family, friends, and church support network.

My next career opportunity was to work in product development, the lifeblood of the business. Seeing how new vehicle-product programs were developed and executed was a great learning experience. I then spent time in product strategy where I met my second business mentor, Mark Malcolm, who would become a friend and tennis partner. We worked together on a benchmark-driven product program target structure that ended up being adopted by the company. It got great exposure with senior management, all the way up to the board.

With that visibility, I was introduced to a couple of Ford legends, Arjay Miller (former President) and Ed Lundy (former longtime CFO and Henry Ford II confidant), two of the "Whiz Kids", former US Air Force veterans who worked in the management science operation. They were part of a group of ten members who joined Ford after World War II and brought professional management principles and discipline to the company. All ten become senior executives at Ford or other Companies, the most famous being Ed McNamara, Ford President, US Secretary of Defense, and World Bank President.

When I was introduced to these two Ford legends, they were sitting at a conference table by the head of finance. We stood and reached over the table to shake hands, and after the handshake, Ed Lundy looked at me and said, "Kevin, you are a tall man, and that is a competitive advantage in the business world." He then turned to the head of finance and told him, "You've done well for being so short." After my initial shock, I was afraid that this would negatively impact my relationship with the finance head. He did give me some grief for a while, but to my surprise, he sent me a note saying how Ed Lundy was impressed with me and made favorable comments about me to the Ford CEO. I have that note framed in my office to this day.

The Ford culture at the time I started was old school, from office dress to office communication and management structure. Office dress was a blue or gray solid or pinstripe suit with a white or blue dress shirt, along with a solid or striped tie. If you wanted to take a risk, you might go with a paisley tie on a Friday. Office communications were structured and used the writing rules named after Ed Lundy, called "Lundyisms"—a form of proper, formal English usage. You always put on your suit jacket when you went to the management dining room for lunch or to the executive offices.

One time I was called to a meeting in the executive offices, quickly threw on my suit jacket, and headed to the elevator. After exiting the elevator, I quickly made my way down the hall and turned the corner, and to my shock, I ran into the CEO, who was exiting a conference room. On impact, he stumbled back but kept his balance. He looked at me for a moment and then continued down the hall. I thought my career was over, but nothing ever came of it—except he would give me a look whenever I saw him.

On the home front, we were adding to our family, welcoming our second son, John

Gerard. I call him Johnny, but he now officially goes by Jack, and came out of the womb looking like a little man. The birth of your children is a tremendously emotional experience, and every time is special. John was the second great gift my wife and I received, in the form of this little boy who would bring such great joy.

On the work front, I moved from the product development organization to the marketing and sales world. At the time, the sales organization was in the Renaissance Center in downtown Detroit, away from Ford's Dearborn headquarters and engineering base. The building of this center was led by Henry Ford II as an attempt to trigger a renaissance in Detroit and Ford became a major tenant.

Going from working with engineers to salespeople was a major business culture shift and required me to adapt to my new environment. This was one of my favorite jobs, given its real-time focus on the marketplace. I had the responsibility of developing vehicle incentive programs to help hit sales goals, which included customer and dealer rebates, discount financing, and lease programs. I had a daily report card from the marketplace and was constantly evaluating program effectiveness and making adjustments.

In this role, I also had the opportunity to spend time with dealers and get feedback from customers. This also allowed me to tie together my earlier Ford Credit experience, which was an enabler the Sales organization used often to execute our marketing programs. During my tenure, the company experienced a high level of sales success, with Ford boasting five of the top ten vehicles sold in the US.

At the time, the company was one of the largest corporate advertisers, and we leveraged these sponsorships for entertaining. I got to be a host at several sporting events, my favorite being a Super Bowl dealer event in New Orleans, where I escorted Heisman Trophy winner Herchel Walker for an evening. I also met most of the great players from the Packers' previous championship teams. At the Super Bowl itself, Ford awarded a vehicle to the MVP of the game. During that ceremony, I met Heisman trophy winner Desmond Howard. I still have the photo we took with him and a signed game ball in my trophy case, which once I caught my boys throwing around the yard like it was no big deal.

While I was making progress in my career, we also tried to be active in our church. My wife used her gifts with children to lead the kids' ministries while I took on the role of church treasurer for a dozen years. At the same time, we made lifetime friendships of mutual support through good times and bad. Tim and Elaine Duncan had two boys the same ages as ours, and Faye had known Elaine since her high school days working at Baskin Robbins, while Tim and I got to know each other playing on the church softball team.

Although I played travel baseball as a teenager, I was surprised at the level of competitiveness and trash talk going on among grown men in the church league. One time, I hit a ball over the outfield and was running around the bases for a home run when, to my surprise, the catcher was in the base path blocking the plate. Unfortunately, my competitive instincts kicked in and my 225-pound frame met the 5'8", 180-pound catcher. The result looked something like a Marvel movie, as the catcher flew through the air to the backstop,—and I was ejected for lack of sportsmanship! Can you believe it? The only comfort I received was from my brothers, who admitted that they would have done the same.

A big bonding experience with the Duncans was our trip down to Florida in a motorhome with our kids. I learned that Tim liked to drive and play country music, among other things. This was my first time driving a motorhome, and I learned it required constant attention to keep it on the road, so I kept focused with a two-handed grip. Tim, on the other hand, took a much more casual approach; one hand on the wheel while eating a sandwich with the other hand, telling stories about the time he worked in a funeral home. Not sure his driving approach was a smart risk.

On our trip back from Florida, we stopped at the Yogi Bear campground for the night. It was dusk when we pulled in, and we needed to dump our waste tank after a week on the road. I had no experience doing this, so I was looking to Tim to perform the operation. We pulled up to the dump station and Tim hooked it up and turned on the release. Everything seemed to be flowing well for the first five to ten minutes, then we noticed that several feet away something began to hiss and bubble out. We went over to look and realized it was the pressure release valve and the tank was likely full.

Tim quickly turned off the motorhome release, but it was too late to stop the "Volcano," as we watched a slow-motion flow of human lava roll down the hill and onto several adjacent campground sites. Given that it was getting late, most families were inside and did not realize what had happened. To Tim's credit, he went and notified all the campers, who seemed to be in a state of disbelief. We decided not to stay the night and got back on the road. This provided a number of life lessons—and I have not traveled in a motorhome since.

In a strange sort of way, Tim and I bonded on that trip and became the best of friends. It ended up being the first of many trips and adventures for us over several decades, traveling all over the world. Our first big series of trips were our Labor Day weekend backpacking trips. These were led by my friend "Ranger" Pete, along with me, Tim, and other friends from church. These were great for relationship building as we hiked, canoed, rafted, and camped together from the Upper Peninsula of Michigan to Canada to the Smoky Mountains over a decade of weekends. When you spend time in these types of environments, you get to know people in a deeper way and develop lasting friendships.

After our boys got out of diapers, we began our series of father and son weekend trips, an attempt to set aside time to intentionally build relationships with our kids. These would take us from upper Michigan to Paducah, Kentucky and Land Between the Lakes, to Cooperstown and the Baseball Hall of Fame, Mammoth Caves, Las Vegas, Phoenix, and the Grand Canyon. There is some dispute between Tim and the boys and myself about whether or not we ever saw the Grand Canyon. I'm all about taking smart risks, so I swear I would never let my boys hang over the ledge of the Grand Canyon. To this day, when I see an article on people falling off the Grand Canyon, I send a group text reminding them how I saved their lives—and how their wives and kids should be thanking me for my diligence all those years ago.

When you spend decades together in relationship, you find opportunities to share and celebrate the journey together. As part of this, we also had a tradition of thirtieth birthday party roasts, where my brothers and I were skewered about all our previous embarrassing moments, combined with a little kindness at the end. My mother was always the featured speaker, and she would give her "Gospel according to Bee." She was hilarious, making fun of her boys and giving us a chance to relive old times. It was at one of these events that the secret of the "broken picture window" became "public"—which means my dad finally found out for the first time!

Several years earlier, we were throwing a baseball around the living room, and it went through the corner of a large picture window. We quickly went into damage control and covered the hole with plastic, taped it up and put a planter in front. Over the years, my father would remark about feeling a draft on cold windy days, but never knew where it came from. Surprisingly, my dad handled this revelation pretty well and finally had the window fixed —and miraculously, the drafts ceased. Maybe we should have gotten over our fears earlier and saved on years of utility bills.

The early years of my professional career were an excellent learning experience. It gave an opportunity to build skills and help identify areas of interest that provided me with career direction. At the same time, the Redhead and I were starting our family and getting involved in our church and community. We learned that real life is integrated, between family, work, and outside interests that can overlap and at times compete with each other. The key is to learn to manage all these interests while still getting some sleep. Little did we know, however, that our world was about to change significantly, as we began a series of great global adventures.

PART 3

THE INDIANA JONES YEARS

Because Ford was one of the world's largest global companies, getting international experience was encouraged and important for career development. Because of their unique nature, these assignments were life experiences that impacted the whole family. The learnings I gleaned from these experiences could provide enough material for their own book.

One of the immediate things you recognize is that everything seems different from where you came from. Almost daily you feel like Dorothy, saying to yourself (or Toto), "We are not in Kansas anymore." You are out of your comfort zone, with an accompanying sense of both fear and adventure. The key here is the attitude you take when approaching these new situations; either you stay closed, paralyzed by your fears, or you make it an Indiana Jones-style adventure quest. Getting the most learning and enjoyment out of these experiences requires you to immerse yourself in the culture, language, and people. This can obviously be uncomfortable, but I found it's always worth it, and leaning in creates memories and relationships that last for life.

One of the key life lessons I picked up from my international experiences has been how to best approach meeting new people. Unlike when you are at home, these environments are almost always different and unfamiliar. At the same time, developing personal relationships can make all the difference between success and failure on these assignments—both on the job and in your personal life. Many people will not do business or interact with you unless there is a real relationship there, and usually, initial meetings are, either all or in part, "getting-to-know-you" sessions.

Because of the cultural differences inherent in these kinds of relationships, you have to make a focused effort to find a point of connection that you can build from. This means you have to be good at asking questions and finding where there might be a mutual interest. These interests can be in areas like sports, art, food, wine, travel, family, common relationships or people, or experiences—anything that can provide a basis to build from. In my experience, developing this ability to find and build off of a point of connection is non-negotiable.

Another life lesson I learned from these assignments is that you have to know that these are limited in time, so don't miss an opportunity when it appears, because it likely will not come along again. After a while, you learn to be both purposeful in making sure you see and do as much as possible, while also being spontaneous to jump on an opportunity that presents itself. In fact, I've learned that this is the best way to approach life all the time—because you may never have a given opportunity again.

The next four chapters (8-11) highlight our experiences and lessons from traveling the globe and working in three world capitals: Tokyo, Paris, and London. Each of these had some similarities but also a variety of distinct cultural differences and unique experiences to offer, as we packed our bags and followed in Dr. Jones's famous footsteps.

CHAPTER 8

SUMO

"POWER" - THE TEMPTATIONS

My next assignment was a supporting role with Ford Asia-Pacific operations, which were based in Melbourne Australia at the time. During that period, Ford's operations in Asia were primarily in Australia, New Zealand, and Taiwan, where they had manufacturing facilities and a large market share. I took my first of many day-long plane trips to Melbourne to meet the management team. The city was vibrant, with its unique combination of multi-ethnic cosmopolitanism and an obvious Victorian history.

My new colleague met me and took me around the city. We had lunch at the beach, and I was introduced to beach cricket. I also learned that boomerangs really do work. I would eventually see an Australian Rules Football game at the Melbourne Cricket Ground and adopt the Collingwood Magpies as my club team. During my first ten-day trip, I toured operations and met with the Ford Australia President, who would one day become Ford's CEO.

My first assignment was to assist the management team in developing a strategic plan to address Japanese competition. This would require several more trips to Australia. During one of the many return trips, I had the opportunity to attend the Australian Open tennis tournament, one of the four Grand Slam events. Ford was the title sponsor for the event, securing us front-row seats for the Finals. I keep a framed photo of the event in my office to this day. I enjoyed working with the Australian team, they were very friendly, and it was an honor to be invited to numerous "barbies" at their homes.

My next assignment took me to Auckland, New Zealand, the "City of Sails." The beaches were black from the volcano that formed the island and seemingly everyone had a sailboat in the harbor. New Zealand has a population of about five million people and over twenty-five million sheep. Even when having a hamburger, it always seemed to taste like lamb.

Its rugby team, the All Blacks, are the national pride and joy, and the team is always ranked among the world's best. One night, while talking to a colleague at my hotel, a big guy, who seemed to be about forty years old, came up to me and asked if I was a Yank. He must have heard my American accent. After I confirmed his suspicions, he replied that American football was for "sissies" and Rugby was the true sport for tough men. He continued that he used to play for the All Blacks. Given that he was a little drunk and very large, I quickly formulated a comeback. I explained that

American football came from Rugby, and therefore, we are like family. He liked that answer and offered to buy me a drink.

I was in New Zealand to find a partner for one of our automotive components plants. It was built with government tax incentives but struggled to make money with the low local volumes. The major issue was that potential markets were thousands of miles away in Japan and other Asian countries, and the export of products was too costly to be competitive. No one was interested in this business. In some cases, there are no solutions to a problem, and you simply do the best with the hand you are dealt. For this plant, we shifted to maximizing production efficiencies and after-market sales opportunities. We sought further government support while planning an orderly phase out of operations with a focus on minimizing the personal and financial impact.

After I had started my assignment, Ford decided to make a major shift in strategy: Moving its Asian-Pacific office from Melbourne to Tokyo, while strengthening its relationship with Mazda. Previously, Ford had a major presence in the Japanese market, where it was the largest auto company prior to World War II. During the war, Ford's operations were expropriated to support the Japanese military efforts.

After the war, Ford focused its efforts on converting its US operations back to civilian use. Given resource constraints, Ford decided not to go back into Japan, despite encouragement from the occupying US military government to support local employment. As a favor, Ford allowed employees from a former textile equipment manufacturing company to spend several months in its facilities, including the famous Rouge complex, which was a fully integrated, just-in-time manufacturing operation. This included the future Chairman and CEO of that former Loom company, Toyota. The time spent in the Ford complexes gave ample insight to the fledgling company, fostering the creation of its own fully integrated automotive facilities and manufacturing system.

During this period, having an Asian-Pacific operation without a meaningful presence in its largest market, Japan, was a strategic weakness. Ford concluded that taking a controlling interest in Mazda would provide access to their small vehicle engineering expertise and an entry point into the Japanese market. My new assignment was to work with the negotiating team to establish this relationship.

Ford based its Japanese offices in downtown Tokyo near the US embassy. The negotiating team was led by a seasoned executive from Australia who was well-versed in Asian markets. I would soon discover that this would be a master class in negotiating strategy and tactics. I learned that some of the key Western negotiating principles of compromise or a linear point-by-point process were not necessarily practiced in my new environment. A good negotiator needed to understand body language and how to listen carefully to what was said, and, importantly, unsaid.

Negotiations were like a Sumo wrestling match, with a regimented, circular approach, in which power and leverage influence the final outcome. The sessions were long, with only the lead negotiators speaking. Given these negotiations were quite complex and time-consuming, I was required to spend most of my time in Japan while my wife and two small kids remained in the US. When it became clear that these discussions would go on for an extended period of time, Ford agreed to bring my family over for several months. We received a one-bedroom apartment in Tokyo not far from the office. The high-rise building was modern, and the apartment had features you would not see in the US. The bathroom acted like a large shower room with a center drain, and the toilet had a seat cover that rotated after each use. We were on one of the top floors and had a good view of the area, including a Japanese cemetery whose daily visitation activity was a cultural experience to observe.

My wife is a high-energy, "Let's go for it" woman, which was perfect for this type of situation. She was quickly out and about in the city with the kids while I was working. On the weekends, we visited key sites around Tokyo and made a few longer trips via bullet train. One thing I learned was that the trains ran on time, and I needed to duck my head when getting in since they were only six-foot openings. My wife realized that public restrooms in Japan at the time were a hole in the ground, and she tried to avoid them at all costs.

The combination of being a tall, attractive Redheaded woman and having a family of fair-haired children made Faye something of a spectacle (I would say something approaching a goddess). People often asked to touch her hair, practice their English with her, and give the kids gifts. One of the common questions was which TV show was her favorite. Given that all the TV content was in Japanese, the choices were limited to kids' shows and sports, like Sumo. So, her response was Sumo, which was the perfect answer, and in one instance, she was even given tickets to an event.

One of the most interesting experiences was our family trip to Tokyo Disneyland. While the kids were playing near a display of 1950s Americana, with Motown iconic cars including a Chevy Bel Air and Ford Thunderbird, we watched a large crowd of Japanese people leaving the Disney character actors to come see my family. Apparently, the opportunity to meet us was a rarer and potentially more interactive experience. My wife coped with this attention, but admitted she could never hide or blend in—we weren't in Motown anymore.

On the career front, negotiations with Mazda were slow, with apparently little progress. The lead negotiators collectively decided a night out might help with relationship building. Our evening included dinner, drinks, and karaoke, where the Japanese team seemed to loosen up, going from silent to very talkative. It was like flipping a switch.

The highlight was definitely the karaoke, which my new Japanese friends took very seriously. When my turn came, I wanted to sing a Michael Jackson Motown song, but I recalled my wife's constant reminder that I did not have the range for MJ. As Clint Eastwood once said, "A man needs to know his limitations." It pained me, but I knew she was right.

If Michael was off the table, what would I perform? The Temptations' Melvin Franklin was a bass, so songs like "Power" and "Old Man River" where he was the lead singer were obvious choices. Unfortunately, they did not have either of them on the song list. I ultimately decided on Elvis's ballad, "Love Me Tender," and Tony Bennet's "I Left My Heart in San Francisco." I knocked it out of the park—at least, that's how I remember it.

That night was transformational for our negotiation process, and we would go on to have several more relationship-building sessions. A surprising pattern began to form: During one meeting we would agree on a point, then at the next one we would debate the same point again. I learned the key to progress was identifying the things the other side really valued, sometimes relatively minor points to us, but very important to them. Eventually, by conceding on one of these minor points, we made it possible for the other side to agree to the deal.

I made several trips to Hiroshima, the first city that experienced the devastation of the atomic bomb. The Mazda facilities were only three miles away from the epicenter of the explosion, yet they were relatively unaffected because there was a mountain between them. I remember being at Peace Memorial Park, which was built upon an open field created by the atomic explosion, on the anniversary of the event. It was an emotional time, with a mostly Japanese crowd along with a few Westerners.

With a deal framework in place, my assignment was completed, and it was time to return to the States. The agreement with Mazda resulted in Ford taking effective control of Mazda and appointing a Ford executive as CEO. This was the first time a US company controlled a Japanese public company. Ford invested key personnel and resources in Hiroshima and began to integrate product plans with Mazda, establishing a relationship that would last several decades.

At the time, I had no idea that this experience was a prelude to a future, larger role in Japan. On the trip back, we decided to stop in Hawaii for several days. One of the most memorable experiences was the tour of Pearl Harbor and visiting the Arizona battleship memorial where the Japanese had initially attacked. It was ironic that in a short period of time, I visited the places where World War II ended and had begun, at least as far as the United States was concerned. The only thing that was clear when visiting these two places was that there were no winners, only enduring evidence of pain and suffering.

OUR CHILDHOOD HQ

DETROIT PUBLIC SCHOOLS SAFETY BOY

THE FOUR OF US KIDS . . .

. . . AND BIGGER KIDS

OUR FIRST DATE,
HOMECOMING 1976

GARDEN CITY HIGH SCHOOL BASKETBALL
FAYE   KEVIN

OUR WEDDING AND OUR CHARIOT (1970 CHEVY NOVA)

BEE PRAYING AT ST. KEVIN'S MONASTERY, IRELAND

NICK AND BEE AT THE ROMAN COLOSSEUM

NATHAN "NICK" - MY DAD, THE GOLDEN GLOVES BOXER, ALWAYS READY FOR ACTION

A RARE SHOT OF ALL OF US WITH A LONDON
BACKDROP FOR THAT YEAR'S CHRISTMAS CARD

FAYE AND THE
KIDS IN TOKYO
AT TEA CEREMONY

FAYE AND CLAIRE AT
THE EIFFEL TOWER

FAYE AND ME AT THE 2024 PARIS OLYMPICS

MY MENTOR DICK SCHULTZ

MY STAR MUSTANG
("A PIECE OF ART", BIG KENNY'S
"CRANK IT UP GARAGE" TV SHOW)

FAYE & ME AT HITSVILLE

THE JOYFUL DAY I MET MARTHA REEVES

ELLIOT GERARD CRAMTON
LATEST EDITION

OUR FULL FAMILY

CHAPTER 9
AMERICANS IN PARIS

"MY CHERIE AMOUR" - STEVIE WONDER

We'll never forget the love affair of our time working and living in Paris. Cultural immersion enables you not only to learn new things, but it also impacts you in deeper ways that change you forever. Living a life of immersion, being a real player in the game of life, is one of the keys to success and achieving your full potential.

Prior to embarking on our second overseas adventure, we welcomed a third child to the family. When my wife got pregnant, she was worried that we would have a third boy: I came from a family of four boys, and Faye had three brothers, but after a trip to the doctor, my wife came over to the office to surprise me with the news that we were having a girl! We named her Claire, a beautiful French name meaning "clear and bright," which was a perfect name for this amazing first Cramton girl in a generation.

She was given the middle name of Elizabeth, after my mother as well as the Redhead's middle name.

Stevie Wonder wrote "Isn't She Lovely" to celebrate the birth of his first-born daughter, and it makes me feel the same way to this day, especially since this is the song we would later dance to at Claire's wedding.

A few years after our time in Japan, I was approached about an opportunity in France to be the chief financial officer (CFO) of Ford's French 5,000-person operations headquartered in Paris. This exciting potential assignment would mean moving to France with the family for a stay of several years. My wife and I discussed the pros and cons of the assignment, both from a professional and family standpoint, and after talking to trusted friends and a lot of prayer, we decided it was a smart risk to take. It also offered the opportunity to get out of our comfort zone, get immersed in another culture, and learn new things as a family.

The first step in the process was an exploratory trip to meet with the Ford France management team, find schools, and secure housing. On our trip to Paris, we were on a flight with the Ford CEO and his wife, who were visiting their daughter at university. As we waited for our luggage, the CEO's wife was telling Faye how great a life experience this would be for our family and told us to make sure we had a lot of fun. The CEO, who had been quiet while his wife talked, turned to me once she finished talking about fun and reminded me to work really hard!

We visited several schools and settled on the American School in Saint Cloud, across the Seine from Paris, on the site of a former US Army base. The town of Saint Cloud was famous for its connection to Napoleon coming to power after the French Revolution. Now, after finding the school, we began looking for a house somewhere between the school and my office.

During our trip, we stayed at a nice, centrally located hotel in Paris. One night, while having dinner near the hotel, we noticed a couple of young, tall Black women with their mother sitting next to us. As I looked closer, it became clear that these were the Williams sisters, who were in town for the French Open. We weren't the only Americans in Paris. I did not know at that time that the sisters would go on to dominate women's tennis for the next few decades. Later, I had a chance to see them play doubles together at Roland Garros—I still have a photo from that day hanging in my office.

After a few days of touring, we found a house in a town not far from school, near the office. We headed home feeling good about the opportunity.

Once things were confirmed, the complex process of all the logistics and approvals were set in motion. Because of the uncertainty of how long we would be gone, plus the need for more space for three kids, we decided it was a good time to sell our house of a dozen years. We also began the process of an international move, which meant determining what needed to go with you immediately by air, what could come later by boat, and what could stay in the US in storage.

I learned my first French lesson in the power of relationships while securing my work permit. To begin the process, my family and I were required to go to the French consulate in Chicago to apply for the work permit and resident visas. The plan was to start my job in France in a few weeks, followed by my family joining me later. After finishing the application, I asked when it would be approved, and the administrator said it would take several months. I told her I had to start my assignment in a few weeks, and she responded that it was not possible.

We left the consulate and headed for the airport to catch our flight back to Motown. While in the car, I called the HR Director in France about my work permit and visa problems. He told me to delay leaving, and he would get back to me soon. Within thirty minutes, to my surprise, I received a call from the consulate telling me that my work permit and visas were approved. It was only later that I would find out that the HR Director had also been a vice-mayor of a Paris Arrondissement and a friend of former Paris Mayor and then French President Jacques Chirac. It helps to know people in high places!

Although work permits and visas were set, our housing fell through. Because of this, the Redhead took another trip to France by herself to find us a place. Fortunately, she found an even better place near a former royal forest with an abandoned chateau not far from Versailles in La Celle Saint Cloud at 14 Sente du Bois Cloud. The forest would become a magical play area for the kids; I can imagine the Three Musketeers riding through it on their way to meet the King at Versailles.

Unfortunately, our house was not ready when we arrived, so the family lived in temporary housing for a few weeks and began to explore the area. We had to outfit the house with new fixtures (which is common in France) while managing the shipment of our things from America, all of which Faye managed, in addition to getting the family settled and ready to start school, a masterful job of handling change and chaos.

I had started my job several weeks prior to my family's arrival. The Ford France headquarters was a four-story office building with several hundred employees overlooking the Seine River. My office had a view of the river, which was near the area where the Impressionist painters, including Monet and Renoir, had worked in the "plein air" (outdoors in the open air).

Renoir's "Luncheon of the Boating Party" is a favorite of mine (I have a print on my dining room wall), and it was painted near the office at Maison Fournaise, which I visited several times for meals. Given my exposure to the Impressionists while in France, I became a big fan and collected several prints of these artists, including many of their paintings from the area near Paris where I lived and worked. Never in my wildest dreams growing up in Motown did I think life would provide immersion opportunities to experience such things—so beautiful and so different.

We had our first family crisis shortly after moving into our house. The kids were running around, and our youngest son, John (now Jack), fell on the base of the French Doors and cut open his knee. Blood was everywhere, and we were in a panic to get him medical attention. I quickly called my administrative assistant from work for help. She told us where the closest hospital was, and we loaded everyone into the car.

This would begin our traumatic French hospital experience. We got to the emergency entrance, and my wife went in with my son while I parked the car. Given that our French language capability was very basic, and that we had never been in a French hospital, the experience was overwhelming. Fortunately, one of the French doctors was fluent in English, and my wife and son could communicate well enough. Because of the seriousness of his injury, the doctors decided to keep him overnight, and my wife was unable to stay with him. This was crushing for both my son and his mother. Although the injury was less serious than we originally thought, it had a real psychological impact on my son, making him more fearful for several years after the incident.

The kids started at the American School and had a very good experience there. The American community in Paris was welcoming, and my family quickly made new friends. Most of the kids were American expatriates like us, but the school also included other French and International families that wanted an American system education for their children, many of whom would go on to US universities. We got involved in the school and I coached my sons in weekend basketball. We also helped the school with transportation by acquiring discount Ford vans (I personally thought we should drive American at the American School).

The children had access to all the cultural and educational opportunities Paris could offer, including world-class museums and other programs. My oldest son, who had a culinary interest, was able to do a program at Le Cordon Bleu, the famous French cooking school. He also had an opportunity to sing in a boys' choir for unchanged voices (e.g., Vienna Boys Choir) and traveled in Europe giving concerts, allowing him to explore areas where his skills and interests aligned.

The school provided several trips throughout the Paris region and beyond. The highlight was the winter break trip to the French or Swiss Alps for Skiing, a stark difference from the flat terrain near Motown boasting ski hills made from waste sites ("Mount Trashmore").

We also became active in a local church, which had services in both English and French. My wife and I were asked to join the church board and developed some good friendships. We met a Swiss-American family; the dad, Gerard, worked for a division of GM, our historical competitor, and his wife, Karen worked for a computer firm. Our families became close friends, and we had the experience of a lifetime spending Christmas at their chalet in the Swiss Alps. We also invited our Jewish friends from the American School to come to our church to demonstrate Passover, which was a tremendous experience. Building relationships across cultures, ethnicities, and religious backgrounds was a highlight of our time in Paris and was really formative for our family.

We tried to take in French culture and learn the language as well as we could. My wife and I had the same tutor, Edmee Paquet, who became like a mother to my wife, and we became family friends. We later would have the honor of being invited to her son's wedding, which was a true cross-cultural experience.

Learning a language is a great challenge as an adult, since you have to humble yourself into accepting the process, like a child learning to walk by falling and getting up. The difficulty is compounded by the need to build an adult vocabulary in an accelerated timetable. Things that you take for granted at home, like successfully going to the bank and transferring money, were a cause for celebration in France.

Even though I had high school and college French courses, the real-world practice of language reminds me of the difference in sports between practice and playing in a game. Unlike practice, the game is fast, sometimes unpredictable, and requires you to adapt, anticipate, and move on when you make a mistake. So was my French language experience. Although I never became the kind of French speaker that the Académie Francaise would approve of, my daily effort to improve was a key priority.

See, despite being a subsidiary of an American company, the culture and the language of the office was French (although the senior management team all spoke fluent English). This enabled me to begin to understand and navigate the culture while working on my French language skills. My first steps involved trying to speak French at lunch, with my assistant, and in basic conversations, while covering complex subjects in English. I made progress in these areas, including starting to do some presentations in French. My big personal breakthrough was when I began dreaming in French.

My challenge was always vocabulary, and I would often speak "Franglais," a mixture of French and English, to fill in for the French words I didn't know. This was surprisingly reasonably effective as a communication tool. My colleagues were very patient, helpful, and encouraging in my efforts to learn the language—even though I must have been painful to listen to at times.

There were also significant cultural differences in the office that required me to adapt. Every morning at the start of the business day, there was a structured way to greet your colleagues. If you were a male, you would greet your male colleagues once with a firm handshake, and attempting to shake their hand again was a form of insult, since it signaled that you forgot that you had already done it. With women, you would exchange kisses on both cheeks. If you forgot or passed someone by that you knew without a greeting, this was also an insult. Given that there were several hundred people in the office, it would take some time to get from reception to my office.

Another custom was the office coffee regime, which started with a double espresso (café serre) before the workday, a mid-morning coffee break (pause café), and another coffee after lunch, while some would have another mid-afternoon and another with dinner. Given that I didn't grow up with this near-constant infusion of caffeine, I would start to feel my body shake after the third or fourth double espresso—and eventually had to cut back. For many of my colleagues, their activity and engagement levels went up and down, along with their caffeine intake timing.

In the company cafeteria (cantine), you could get wine, beer, selected soft drinks, and bottled water, but no diet Coke (Coca Light). I had them put in a supply for me. Some employees were concerned with the caffeine levels and chemical make-up of Coke, but somehow were unconcerned by the more familiar daily regimen of double expressos?

Most days, I ate lunch either in the management dining room with the senior team or the cantine with the other employees. From time to time, though, we would go out for lunch, or I would have outside business meetings. On one such day, I was at an outside meeting and missed the lunch period, so I stopped on my way back to the office at McDonald's and brought it back to work. This became one of the biggest scandals of my time in France.

Upon coming into the office with my bag of McDonalds, the reception staff immediately began alerting the whole building of the violation. There was talk of the need for a professional fumigation service to rid the building of the odor. So, to avoid being permanently canceled, I had to commit to no further food violations.

My French colleagues told me they had never been to McDonalds and could not imagine ever going, whereas my American kids needed their McDonald's fix, so we would go on weekends. On one occasion, we ran into a couple of my colleagues who were there with their own kids. Clearly, they were embarrassed that they had been caught, and told me it was the "premiere fois" or "first time!" We went on to have a nice discussion in French, and by the end, they were complimenting me on my language progress.

I went home and told my wife about the encounter and how my colleagues mentioned my French language progress. It was at that time that my son, Nathan, said, "Dad, what do you expect? You sign their paychecks." It was not the first or last time my family would provide me with a needed dose of humility!

One of early cultural tests at the office was understanding the sanctity of the French summer vacances (vacation), a consecutive four-week period during late July/early August. I was taught that the psychology of French vacation was that the first week was to unwind from work, and the last was to gear back up, so only the two weeks in the middle were totally restful. It turns out the only times Americans have a real vacation is when they're in school or after they retire.

My boss was going on vacation and handed me a sealed envelope with his contact details, saying not to contact him unless absolutely necessary. Upon his return four weeks later, I handed him back the sealed envelope— cultural test passed!

Unlike the US, where most people are exposed to sports and team activities at school, the French system was individual achievement focused on the fundamentals of reading, writing, math, and science, founded on the Military structure from the Napoleonic era. Sports, arts, theater, music, and more were primarily pursued outside of the formal French school system.

Furthermore, students were very focused on government-testing success around those fundamental subjects that determined their future university and career prospects. One of my colleagues had a son who was ill and missed some school. When he returned to school, he had difficulty getting his fellow students to share notes, because everyone was viewed as a competitor for university placement—not a teammate.

Not surprisingly, this school experience also impacted the office culture, as professional employees were very comfortable working individually in their offices with doors closed. One early mistake I made was assigning a team project and expecting that the members would get together and make progress until the next review date. I quickly learned that I needed to act as a facilitator and model team behavior to teach them how to play together. This process took time, and some employees were better and quicker learners than others.

While I liked a very participative meeting approach, allowing lower-level employees to attend and present at meetings, the office culture was more of a traditional hierarchical environment. Senior meetings tended to include functional heads only, featuring frequent lunch meetings with a multi-course meal, including wine, in the management dining room, where key decisions were made. Again, I had to adapt to the culture, but I thought it was important to find opportunities for my team members to participate and develop. I found special projects were a good way to get my team development and exposure opportunities. I also kept my team briefed after key meetings, which was appreciated and efficient for supporting follow-up assignments.

The management team spent a lot of time together, and in an effort to improve effectiveness, we had an outside expert come in to facilitate some team-building activities. The consultant was an expert in psychology and the functions of the brain. The weeklong session was all in French, and I ended up with a headache after each day. The truth is that I would have struggled to fully understand the discussions on brain function if they had been in English, never mind in French.

As part of these activities, we did a standard personality test. I had done several of these before, and the results were similar, highlighting my strong analytical bent. It was the results of my colleagues that were surprising, who all scored as perfectly balanced in all areas. It turns out that they had completed the test based on how they would like to be, what they aspired to. If I had known that was the expected approach to the test, I would have answered as Michelangelo— the perfect Renaissance man, painter, sculptor, and architect.

One of the key business culture differences were the relationships in France between big government and large corporate businesses. In several instances, the government would have shareholdings in French businesses, often encouraging employees to move between government and corporate jobs through various stages of their careers, with government officials making or influencing key decisions.

This structure influenced French career decisions, including the phenomenon of top college graduates aspiring to government positions. In the US, those same students would be looking at tech, start-ups, consulting, banking, private equity, or large corporations, with government roles not even on the list for consideration. It was only after I met a colleague and her son for lunch at the treasury offices that I got a better understanding of the influence and career positioning that these government experiences offered—plus, you got to eat in the dining room of a former Royal Palace.

The French government often put in place laws that drove business behavior, many times in ways they did not anticipate. One law was the thirty-five-hour work week (trente-cinq heures), which was, in theory, an effort to create more jobs, but the higher cost and inflexibility of labor accelerated the drive for efficiency and automation. The government was serious about making sure business adhered to these requirements, and one executive at another company was detained when a raid of the office found people working beyond the legal requirements. My colleagues, to mess with me, would say that the government liked to make examples of executives from American companies ... and that I could be next!

Because of the inflexibility of making workforce changes and the high cost of reducing employment, the company was very careful in hiring new full-time employees. This created an interesting dynamic in the office, since we used college interns for up to a year to staff most of the entry-level positions. This resulted in an office make-up of mostly long-tenured people thirty-five years and older and a rotating group of twenty-year-olds, which created its own challenges. Managing this type of demographic structure, with experienced employees constantly training new employees for entry-level positions, could be tricky.

Understanding the environment you are entering into is critical for successful engagement. Once you know the rules, it is easier to play the game, which is why the upfront work that is inherent in taking smart risks is so important, knowing you will need to react and adapt as your understanding increases or when circumstances change. Knowing your environment also helps develop those points of connection that are critical to building lasting personal relationships.

My foray into wine was one of my cultural and business immersion efforts. Ford built its first Model-T plant on the European continent in Bordeaux, France, and during my time, Ford was the largest private employer in Bordeaux, the leading wine region in France, which offered employees a special discount on purchases. This was an opportunity I could not pass up, so we built a substantial wine cellar at my French house.

Furthermore, our Legal Director was a vintner (winemaker) and owned a wine-producing estate in the Loire Valley, south of Paris. As a vintner, he was a member of the Paris Wine Club, including most of the winemakers in France, who kept a supply of their wine stored at the Club. He would invite us from time to time for dinner and to sample wines there, which was one of my favorite experiences and solidified my love for wine and French culture.

My family had the opportunity to visit his chateau in the Loire Valley, a 1000-year-old castle surrounded by a moat and slots in the walls used to fire arrows at invaders. Artisans lived on the Chateau site until the 1960s, reflecting centuries of French village culture in which the Church and Chateau anchored the town. These were indelible experiences that made us feel transported back in time.

I also built a good relationship with our HR Director, who was great at cutting through the "red tape" of the French bureaucracy and helped me and my family out often. He was one of the best-connected people I have ever met, with great relationships both inside the company, including former Chairman and CEO Henry Ford II (who loved to visit Paris), and with the French government, not to mention members of the arts and media. In recognition of his service to France in these many facets, he was awarded "the Ordre National du Merite" by his friend, President Jacques Chirac. My wife and I were privileged to attend the ceremony and congratulate my friend and colleague for his lifetime of service.

One of the most significant team-building experiences while I was in Paris was the World Cup soccer tournament (la Coupe de Monde) hosted in France. The company had a box at the national stadium, Stade de France, for the whole multi-week tournament. Now, I grew up in the US before the soccer revolution, and I never played or seriously followed the sport. Because of this, I was totally ignorant of how important this tournament was to fans around the world.

I had a block of tickets assigned to me and thought it would be a good idea to take a few of my key team members to a match, which I discovered was that next to offering them the keys to heaven, providing someone with a ticket to a World Cup match was a close second. I have never experienced a greater or longer lasting appreciation from those team members, especially since the French team captured the cup that year. My boys also became enamored with soccer during that time, played the game, and became lifetime fans—and to this day, they get up early in the US to watch the European premiere League matches. It was only later, when I watched Lionel Messi play for a friend's team in the US, that I better understood the universal power of the sport.

Because I was the senior American from a prominent company, I was invited often to activities hosted by the American Chamber of Commerce and the US Embassy. At these events, I got to meet colleagues from other large American companies in France, including Disney, GE, and IBM. Some of these people I knew through the American School or church, so it became a great opportunity to get together. One of the guys we met through church was in Paris leading the animation for Disney on the movie "Tarzan," which was an amazing coincidence considering how much the "Tarzan" animated character looked like the assistant pastor at our church.

One of the most unique experiences was attending a new movie premiere in Paris of *A Chance or Coincidence*. This movie was made by the iconic French director Claude Lelouch, who won an Academy Award for his film *A Man and a Woman*, and featured a Mustang convertible. At the theater entrance for the premiere, we had a classic Ford Mustang convertible along with some sporty new models on display. I had a chance to meet the director and walked on the "red carpet" that was laid down at the entrance of the theater.

Much like my Asian experience, developing relationships in France usually took time and required shared experiences. Although my French colleagues were friendly at work and we had team events outside the office, it was rare to get an invitation to dinner at someone's home. Unlike the US, where there is often a blending between work and private life, in France, there was clearly a separation, and private life (vie privee) was closely guarded.

In France, it was a privilege to be invited to a dinner party at someone's home. The host would make a great effort in selecting the multi-course menu and often agonize over optimal wine pairings. A formal French dinner would have up to seven courses (starter, soup, fish dish, entrée, which is the meat course, sorbet, salad, cheese, and finally, dessert). Seating was important, and couples were often separated to encourage discussions with others during dinner. These events would last hours and provided an opportunity to build or deepen relationships.

We tried to experience as much as possible with the family during our stay in France. On Sundays, we would go to church and then head to the boulangerie (or bakery) for fresh baguettes that we would consume on our way home. Frequently, we would stop at the French street market by the train station near our house for rotisserie chicken and fresh vegetables. My wife would put together a picnic lunch; we'd load up our bikes, and then head to the Château of Versailles. We would have lunch and then take a leisurely bike ride around the property. Claire learned to ride her bike at the train station parking lot and would perfect her skills riding around the gardens of Versailles. Paris was a world unto itself, but it was also our home-away-from-home base for adventures that would take us to every corner of France and a number of unforgettable destinations across Europe, the Mediterranean, Africa, and the Middle East.

CHAPTER 10

ALL OVER THE MAP

"CRUISIN'" - SMOKEY ROBINSON

Traveling and experiencing new places, cultures, and people is one of the greatest opportunities in life to build relationships, explore your interests, take smart risks, and really live in the moment. As a family living abroad, we were committed to doing something new around town every week, as well as a trip further afield once a month. Like the well-traveled Dr. Jones, we found ourselves all over the map, both literally and figuratively. Having the opportunity to see and learn new things is one of the greatest joys in life. Once, we decided to take a car trip to the south of France, but my colleagues were shocked when I told them we planned on going by car. Unlike Americans, who often travel cross-country by car, my colleagues preferred to go by train or if there was enough distance, by plane. We learned that train travel is preferred because the road system is not like the standardized US interstates and traversing all the smaller towns and city centers took forever.

The diverse topography and beautiful vistas of France were highlights of the trip. We also had the opportunity to practice our French, as fewer people spoke English the further away we traveled from Paris. The people in the countryside were appreciative and very forgiving of our French language skill limitations. We stayed in castles, manor houses, and farms on our way. Over the course of several days, we made it to Nice on the French Riviera and enjoyed the beach, then returned via a different route.

French swimwear and beach attire is much different than in America and took some time to get accustomed to. Most French pools required men to wear a short brief Speedo for sanitary reasons, not the baggy style suits I was familiar with. Olympic athletes look good in these swimsuits; dad bodies not so much—which my daughter liked to remind me of. She told me that she wouldn't come to the pool if I wore the Speedo. I still have it, hoping one day, perhaps foolishly, that I can get back in Olympic shape.

My favorite trip we took while in France was a ten-day Mediterranean cruise. My only previous cruise experience was the Boblo boat during my youth in Motown, which ferried us to the Boblo island amusement park on the Canadian side of the Detroit River, as we listened to old music, drank Faygo pop, and ate hotdogs, peanuts, and popcorn.

The Mediterranean cruise was almost canceled due to some security issues, especially concerning Israel and Egypt, and all the Americans except one other family dropped out. We decided that the combination of the beefed-up armed security and the fact that the Europeans were going ahead made the trip an acceptable risk to take.

We started our voyage departing from the French Riviera, traveling down the Italian coast to Capri and then on to Sicily. Once there, we went to the top of Mount Etna, which was an active volcano at the time. It was ninety degrees at the base, but there was fresh snow at the peak. We witnessed the structures that had been enveloped by recent volcanic activity as we made the climb. At the top, we stood on the rim of a dormant volcano crater with the wind blowing so hard we had to hold on to the kids to keep them from flying away.

From Sicily, we headed across the Mediterranean to Alexandria, Egypt, founded by Alexander the Great, one the greatest intellectual and cultural centers in history. We then traveled to Cairo, stopping first at the Egyptian Museum to see King Tut. From there, we visited the Sphinx, the famous spiritual guardian statue of a man with a pharaoh headdress and a lion's body.

Our next stop was the Great Pyramid of Giza, the only remaining wonder of the ancient world. At the Great Pyramid, we ignored our tour guide's instructions and went into the burial chamber of Pharaoh. My son darted ahead of me down a dark, angled shaft about five feet high, which required me to bend down to follow. It was a forty-five-degree angle down, so I had to hold on to the ropes on each side to avoid falling. As I continued down the shaft, I became terribly claustrophobic and could not see the end of the tunnel. It felt like I would never get to the burial chamber.

Once I finally arrived in the dimly lit chamber, I could see where the torches once were placed, and the room smelled like it was truly five thousand years old. We walked around exploring the area like Indiana Jones and came upon the place where the Pharaoh's sarcophagus was once laid, where my son and I laid down and pretended we were Pharaoh. Our way out went much quicker—like we were walking on air. As we exited the shaft glowing with accomplishment, my wife snapped a picture that would become one of her favorites to this day.

Our next destination was Israel. Surprisingly, one of the first things we saw after arriving was an Elvis Presley billboard. The main priority was to visit all the Holy Sites. It was emotional walking down the Via Dolorosa, the same path many believe Jesus took to his crucifixion. We observed people praying and tucking in notes in the stones at The Wailing Wall, the Western Wall of the Temple. When we visited the Mount of Olives, it was preserved in a way so that you can envision yourself there two thousand years ago, with ancient olive trees surrounding you as you look down at the Garden of Gethsemane, where Jesus prayed. We traveled to Bethlehem, the birthplace of Jesus, which felt more like a tourist spot than a manger scene. It was the only place we felt at risk, as several local men were walking around asking if Americans were on the tourist buses. We decided to keep a low profile.

After Israel, we headed to Cyprus, which is partially governed by both Greece and Turkey. We then moved on to the Greek Isles and Rhodes, which at one time hosted the Colossus statue. The crusaders under the Knights of St. John were headquartered in Rhodes and governed the island for over two-hundred years. The Palace of the Grand Master of the Knights of Rhodes felt like the set of an *Indiana Jones* movie waiting for the knights of the "Last Crusade" to walk down the halls.

The next stop was Athens, where you can see the famous Acropolis from the harbor. I raced my two boys in the one-hundred meters at the Olympic stadium–it was surprisingly close and ended my sprinting career. Our final destination in Greece was Mount Olympus, where we watched an ancient ceremony and felt like we were a part of Greek Mythology.

While our Mediterranean cruise was magical, one of our trips back to France from Christmas holidays was harrowing. We had a huge snowfall in Motown the day before heading back to Paris, which delayed our departing flight for several hours. The five of us were traveling together, resulting in ten checked bags filled with books, presents, canned goods, hard-to-find American food items, like Oreos, and baking items, like cake mixes.

Once we were in the air, the captain made us aware that we would be diverted to London, since the crew was timing out and could not fly the extra thirty to forty-five minutes to Paris. This created a near-riot on the plane. To calm the passengers, the pilot said we would all be rebooked to Paris and our boarding passes would be available upon landing. That was an outright lie.

When we landed, we found out the airline had done nothing to rebook our flights. We were told to collect our ten heavy bags and get into a long line for rebooking. The other passengers were visibly tired and upset at the airline's incompetence. Eventually, one of the employees yelled out that there was a flight departing for Paris in thirty minutes on a first come basis and to leave our bags and go to the gate. I wanted to run for it, but the

Redhead made it clear that there was no way we were leaving our bags and running with our three kids to the gate. I was not happy, but my wife turned out to be the Prophetess, as the passengers that ran for the gate came back later without making the flight. The lesson learned: Always listen to your wife's instincts.

We finally got to the counter and were booked on a flight to Paris several hours later. Since the only seats available were in economy, the airline refused to allow us into the lounge to wait, which enraged me. Between my anger and the kids' crying, the airline finally acquiesced and let us in.

We finally arrived in Paris almost thirty-two hours later, and we were completely exhausted. We found a taxi van, which could handle, just barely, our ten bags and five passengers. Unfortunately, the driver took the long way to our house, likely to maximize his fare.

Once home, we noticed that it was cold inside. Upon checking the thermostat, it was set at the right temperature, but the house was about fifty degrees, just slightly warmer than the forties outside. When I went down to the basement to check the furnace, it appeared that we had run out of heating oil, and since it was a weekend, it would be several days before we could get a delivery. The Redhead came up with the only viable plan: Everyone would stay in our bedroom with all our blankets and our one space heater. We all loaded into our room, closed the door, and nodded off to sleep, the only good news being that our nightmare trip home was over.

Although we eventually traveled all around Europe, most of our travels were relatively local, consisting of visits to key sites within train or driving distance of Paris. Unsurprisingly, we had a number of visitors during our time in France. Faye, who was a former tour guide at the Henry Ford Museum and Greenfield Village, led most of the trips to Paris and its great Museums. My two favorites were the Louvre, with the "Mona Lisa" and the "Birth of Venus," and the Musee d'Orsay, with its great Impressionist collection.

We lived a few blocks from the train station, which was a direct line into central Paris and facilitated all of these local excursions. The journey had a breathtaking view of the Eiffel Tower rising across the Seine River as the train came around the bend into Paris.

The Redhead also led our trips to the Loire Valley and its famous Chateaus, including "Sleeping Beauty's" castle. My tour guide expertise was Normandy, including the D-Day Beaches and Monet's Garden with its Japanese Bridge and water lilies at Giverny.

We continued our father-and-son bonding weekends with a trip to Normandy, along with our friends, the Duncans, where we stayed at a farm not far from the coast. The owners of the farm did not speak English, so we spoke French exclusively, with a little "Franglais" mixed in to fill in some of my missing vocabulary. We spent the bulk of our trip touring the beaches and the remnants of the World War II fortifications, including the German "Pill Boxes" from which they fired on the Allied Troops. The French people in this part of France were very friendly to Americans, likely because of the daily reminders of the sacrifices that were made to free them from the Nazis.

The trip to the American Cemetery featured in movies such as *Saving Private Ryan* is difficult to put into words properly.

The cemetery is on a cliff above the beaches where the D-Day assault took place. Before entering, we walked along a path from the parking lot lined with tall trees on each side for some distance. At the end of the path, the entrance opens to a breathtaking view of 10,000 white crosses mixed with a few Stars of David. I was immediately wrapped up in emotion as I looked from left to right at the rows upon rows of Americans who made the ultimate sacrifice. I believe every American should experience this moment.

A family friend visited with his father who landed at Omaha Beach on D-Day. As they walked on the beach, my friend asked his father, "Does it look any different than when you were here?" He replied, "The last time I was here, I was trying to stay alive and not looking at the scenery." As my friend's father approached the entrance to the cemetery, he could not go in and went back to the car. He later said he lost too many of his buddies there and couldn't bear to go in, wondering why he was the one who had survived the ordeal.

Of our visitors, none were more special than my parents, who had never traveled outside the US except to Canada. It is incredibly difficult to describe what it is like to live in a foreign country. Photos, TV shows, movies, or even short visits can't fully capture what day-to-day living is like. I was so pleased to have my parents stay at our house, walk to the bus stop with our kids, go to the market, and stroll around the neighborhood. The cultural differences between Motown and Paris were surprising to them, but this visit gave them a new appreciation of what life was like for my family and more context when we would catch up with them on the phone.

My mother had on her wish list a trip to Lourdes, which Catholic pilgrims have visited for over one hundred years. Unfortunately, I had to work, so the Redhead agreed to take my parents by train. My mom was elated, and my dad went along for the ride. My father was an inflexible traveler who demanded the familiarity of his American routine. To start the day, he needed a full English breakfast, not the continental style offered in France. The crushing blow was that the McDonald's was miles away, and in France, they didn't do breakfast at all.

Faye, not being Catholic, planned to take and drop off my mother at the site where you are immersed in the pools of water. Before long, though, my wife was separated from my mother and swept into the process of immersion in the pools. It was an orderly process facilitated by a group of gentle women who seemed to speak the various languages of the pilgrims. As she went into the pool, she could hear beautiful music sung in multiple languages and felt a sense of peace. For this Baptist girl, it was a surprisingly enjoyable experience. My mother was simply joyous, and mentioned she recognized a hymn in Polish from her youth while entering the water.

When we weren't traveling, most of our efforts were to get into a normal family and work routine. One of the best ways to know you are truly familiar with your environment is being able to arrive on time. Because of the heavy Parisian traffic, it was acceptable to be fifteen to thirty minutes late for a meeting or event. In the early days I could easily get lost, so I built in a buffer, but as I got more experienced, I *mostly* arrived early. One of the wild cards was getting caught in a strike action (un greve), which seemed like a French national pastime. The French were supportive of labor actions even if it inconvenienced them personally—perhaps a legacy of revolutionary activity over the years.

One day while heading into work, the construction workers were striking in front of the road to the office. The road was getting backed up, as they would not let anyone through. I waited about thirty minutes with no movement, and since this was unplanned and I had a cup of coffee at home, my bladder told me this had to end. I put my Explorer, which in France is bigger than most of the vehicles on the road, into four-wheel drive and went through the barricades into the office parking lot. The strikers took a couple of steps toward the office but stopped as I got out of the vehicle, likely not wanting to pick a fight with me.

The Explorer also came in handy driving around the city, which was an ongoing game of chicken. A favorite of mine was ruling the traffic circle around the "Arc de Triomphe," where I would drive around ten or more times before heading down the Champs-Elysees.

I must thank Renault for my perpetual French driver's license since when they owned Motown-based American Motors (former owner of the Jeep brand), they entered into a reciprocal driver's license arrangement between France and the State of Michigan—so, no driving test was required of me. This license would be invaluable in France and would be good anywhere in the European Union. The beauty is that, at the time, the European systems were not fully electronically integrated, so I may or may not still have a few outstanding tickets.

After a few years in France, we were hitting our stride. The family had settled well, the school and church provided great friendships, and we began to know our neighbors and the local community. My job was going well, and I was accepted by my colleagues as one of the family. We had made progress in our French language skills, and although far from perfect, we were comfortable functioning within a French environment.

One of the major benefits of these types of assignments is to experience once-in-a-lifetime opportunities. Because these opportunities are fleeting, I grew more comfortable with jumping in, since they will likely not come around again. I've come to realize that we should approach every day with this same level of willingness and proactivity.

It was at this time I was approached about a promotional opportunity in London. This would require another big move, just as my family had grown comfortable in their surroundings. My wife especially loved Paris and was hesitant to move again. Unfortunately, this type of situation is standard for the expatriate life, and we knew coming in that this Paris assignment would be for a limited duration.

The Redhead and I went through our decision process, which is a combination of assessing the pros and cons, praying for guidance, and getting good counsel. We concluded that we were up for another overseas assignment and that London interested us as a family. I felt that if we had to leave Paris, London was the next best alternative. The UK had the advantages of a common language and heritage, but the move would still require us to start all over again, testing all of our skills in decision making and relationship building. As we said "au revoir" to Paris, we left with incredible friendships and memories that would last a lifetime.

CHAPTER 11
ABBEY ROAD

"YOU REALLY GOT A HOLD ON ME"
- BEATLES & SMOKEY ROBINSON

Next to the US, the UK was the most familiar environment we've lived in. London is unique as the political, financial, and cultural capital of the nation and a favorite of foreign nationals from around the world.

After our Paris experience, we expected the transition to London to be easier—but we were wrong. Although there was a similar language and culture, breaking into a new societal structure is always difficult. On its face, things appeared familiar in London, but in many ways, they were not. Unlike our situation in Paris, where our small American community was very welcoming and sympathetic to newcomers, London had a more broadly dispersed expat community, and the local British folks were not quick to embrace us. In retrospect, this should not have been surprising, since most cultures require a period of transition to build relational capital and learn the rules of their society. This immersion process takes time and effort but is the only way to cultivate a meaningful life experience.

The main rule for these family transitions was to first find the kids' school and then our house. In Paris, the most viable school choices were relatively close to one another, not fundamentally impacting the location of our home. In London, though, the choices were either local public or private British schools near the office or the American school in central London, forty minutes away. Unlike Paris, where we were the only American family, the company had multiple families from the US stationed in London.

Most of those families put their kids in the British schools near the office. One of those was a very expensive school attended by many of the wealthy British families. The buildings looked like they could have been at Oxford or Cambridge, which many of the students would go on to attend. My wife did not view this as a good fit; instead, we toured a public school with a more international focus for my older middle-school son and a traditional British private grade school for the younger kids.

Based on trusted recommendations, we went with these two schools and found a house a few miles away. The house was a Tudor-style new build not far from the office. My family was able to move in before school started, and I followed later after a few weeks of transition.

The Redhead was the glue that kept all these transitions moving forward, and she was getting the house in shape, launching the kids at school, and finding us a local church to attend—all at the same time. For the younger kids, the school was a very traditional English prep school with uniforms that was focused on the educational fundamentals. My children looked the part of British school kids and quickly, likely as a defense mechanism, developed a good English accent and began spelling words the British way. My son John's accent got so good that he played the part of King John in the school play. Several people in the audience were amazed when they heard him speaking with his English accent, saying, "Isn't that the American boy?" All in all, my younger kids seemed to make good progress in integrating into their school. My wife, much to her surprise, took some time to get networked into the school moms' group, but made quick progress in building relationships at the local church.

On the other hand, my older son struggled with integration into the British public school. He was teased for being an American and had difficulty breaking into the social structure. After several months, he was miserable and looking for a change. Given the choices, the only viable alternative was the American School in central London, but this was forty minutes away by train.

After we toured the school, my son felt that this was a good fit, and he was willing to do the required commute. At first, we were hesitant to put a middle schooler on a long train ride each day, but he was adamant about not wanting to go back to the British school. So, we let him do it, but it did require him to be productive with his schoolwork on the train. He also developed an amazing ability to do impressions of all the various types of people he saw on the train and could do a whole voice routine.

One of the great life experiences we had as a family was being at the base of Big Ben in London at midnight when the millennium turned to the year 2000. The crowd was huge, the fireworks were incredible, and the celebration was loud. Fortunately, we were able to navigate the crowd, with my daughter Claire sitting on my shoulders. We welcomed in the new year, and the new millennium, with hope and wonder for what it would bring our family in the years to come.

On the job front, I took over a position that oversaw all the European business development merger and acquisition (M&A) activity. It was a busy time, with efforts in acquiring and running European dealerships, buying a Formula 1 team and other racing companies, integrating the Premium Auto Group companies of Jaguar, Land Rover, Aston Martin, Volvo, and Lincoln, developing technology ventures for in-vehicle communications/telematics, and acquiring and building out a European electric vehicle company.

After previously spending time in Ford's marketing and sales group, it was very interesting to get involved in the dealership business, which had a direct interface with the customers. I was one of two Ford board members who oversaw the European dealer group, which included about half of Ford's UK dealerships, Bordeaux, France, and Vienna, Austria. The dealer distribution business' key revenue drivers were service, finance and insurance, and used vehicle sales—very different from the new vehicle production business. Familiarity with this model would help understand what the end customer was looking for in an overall purchase and ownership experience. This distribution model was one I would encounter in future businesses.

At the time, Ford had constructed a fully integrated Formula 1 Racing Team under the Jaguar Racing name, which included engine developer Cosworth Racing and racing electrics provider Pi Technologies. The F1 Team was purchased from racing legend Jackie Stewart, who remained a board member, and the team manager was former champion Niki Lauda.

F1 racing attracts a celebrity crowd at most of the races and is very international in scope, with venues throughout the world. It's also an expensive sport to compete in at the highest levels. Because of this, I was tasked to help find a partner to share the cost. Working with the company president, we came to a tentative deal with energy drinks company Red Bull to form a joint venture. Unfortunately, we could not get a final agreement signed, and I was tasked to find a buyer for the team.

Along with our investment bankers, we looked at several potential candidates and ended with three finalists, including a Russian Oligarch, a Chinese government entity, and Red Bull. "F1 Supremo" Bernie Ecclestone would call me with his suggested buyers, and after some deliberation, we selected Red Bull. The final negotiations were interesting, as I met the founder, Dietrich Mateschitz, at his airplane Hanger-7 in Salzburg, Austria, with its vintage planes and the Red Bull logo all over the place. We pulled an all-nighter with his team to get to a final agreement, including the consumption of gallons of Red Bull energy drinks to keep us awake.

At this time, we were making a foray into e-commerce and in vehicle digital communications or telematics, which included a lot of partnership development activities. It was at this time I began working with my British mentor, John Hitcham, who was a seasoned European marketing executive. John was my "Henry Higgins," educating me in British culture and how to speak proper Oxford (or the Queen's) English, correcting my spelling, pronunciation, and word usage. Beyond that, he was a wise business executive, and I often sought his advice on key issues. We often traveled together across Europe, and he was constantly tutoring me on European history and culture. John also knew all the best restaurants in London, so we enjoyed countless culinary experiences together.

To get scale and access technology, we spent a lot of time developing partnerships and joint ventures. One telematics venture I worked on included all the Ford-owned brands in Europe: Ford, Jaguar, Land Rover, Volvo, Aston Martin, and Mazda, plus the addition of competitors Renault and PSA (now Stellantis). As we integrated these operations, I served as interim President of our Munich, Germany-based unit as well.

With all the premium brands Ford owned at the time, there were efforts to find integration and scale opportunities, and telematics was one area where we had some success. They also made efforts to use common e-commerce platforms. It was interesting to work with all the different brands and their business cultures, but the challenge was to find points of connection where we could build trust and relationships to develop common solutions that could benefit everyone.

One of the big benefits of these premium brands was that my company car was a Jaguar, which just seemed right for cruising around London. Even though I loved the Aston Martins, the Redhead said there was no way I was going to be driving around England pretending to be James Bond.

These were the early days of electrification, and we acquired a European start-up electric vehicle company to accelerate our efforts and help meet government requirements, a business model driven by government incentives and regulation. Our best success was in Norway, which had special lane access, free parking with charging stations, and electric vehicle tax credits, while at the same time having high taxes on petrol vehicles—which heavily influenced the customer decision process. The high cost of electric vehicles, however, especially the battery, made it difficult to offer a price point near a petrol vehicle without incurring a large loss, and many governments in Europe were supportive of purchasing an electric vehicle fleet, but had no appetite to pay for the higher costs.

With all the various work projects going on, I was constantly traveling around Europe. On one fateful day, I was flying into Paris and witnessed the crash of the Concorde supersonic passenger plane at Charles de Gaulle Airport. It was almost surreal as we circled above the burning crash site for 30 minutes as the authorities were trying to determine what to do with the incoming flights into the airport. After over 3 million flight miles, I am always amazed at the miracle of flight and at the same time how catastrophic a failure can be to the passengers on board.

During my time in London, the Company sent me to the Executive Development program at the London Business School. It was a multiple-session program over the course of a year, made up mostly of senior executives from the UK and Europe. It was excellent to interface with other executives from other industries while learning and growing alongside them. Aside from the classroom work, we went out together to build relationships, and I would stay in contact with some of my former classmates many years later.

I had a good team in Europe, including a colleague, Vitaliy Podolskiy, who was born in Ukraine, raised in Russia, and served in the Red Army, where he was the national fencing champion. He studied in the US at the University of Chicago and had worked in consulting, so he was well-equipped for the job. One Monday, he came into the office and seemed a little down. When I asked how he was doing, he responded by asking me if I saw the summer Olympic games over the weekend. I told him that I had and noticed that the Russians won the fencing gold metal. He then responded, "I beat him."

It was clear that he was disappointed that he might have been an Olympic champion and a national hero, but instead was working for me in London. We've stayed in touch over the years, and he has become a highly successful businessman, while that Olympic fencing champion he beat later became head of the Russian Olympic Federation. We still have the fencing foil that he gifted us in a place of honor in our sports memorabilia collection.

The UK was a great place for sports lovers, having been involved in the founding of such sports as golf, tennis, rugby, cricket, rowing, boxing, horse racing, Formula One (F1), and football (soccer). I had the opportunity to attend events at all the major venues, with my favorites being Wimbledon for tennis, Twickenham for rugby, Lords for cricket, Silverston Circuit for F1, and Wembley Stadium for football.

It also helped that Ford was a major sports advertiser and the main sponsor for Champions League Football. We enjoyed going to the matches of our favorite local team, Arsenal, who at the time had several French national team players that we knew.

To this day, my boys have remained Arsenal fans because of their time in London.

Additionally, the dealership group I oversaw was a major sponsor of West Ham United, located east of London close to the major historic Ford facility in Dagenham. The British love their football, and there is no better example of this than our suite at the stadium, which could be rented out for a honeymoon night and was equipped with a pull-down bed and field view. The team now enjoys the former Olympic stadium as their home field.

One of my teenage dreams was to be able to play club tennis with excellent coaching, which was something my parents couldn't afford while I was growing up, and living in London provided me with the ability to give my kids the tennis development opportunity I never had—or so I thought.

One night after work, I went to see my kids practicing at the club. I asked my wife how they were doing, and she said they hated it and were only doing it because of me. Initially this was a surprise and disappointment, but after processing it, I concluded that I was asking my kids to live my dream, and this only works if they really want it themselves. After that, I reluctantly adjusted my parenting, and although I was not shy to provide input, I tried to stay away from forcing things on them that they didn't want.

My oldest son ended up playing rugby, a popular sport in the UK among prep school kids and a sport I knew little about, which is probably one reason he liked it. They struggled against most of the top British schools but did well when they played the other American and International Schools around Europe. He also joined the choir and continued pursuing his interest in music, having the opportunity to perform at Saint Paul's Cathedral and other venues and going on to be a lead singer in a band later in high school.

It was a combination of my oldest son's long commute and my second boy finishing up at the British grade school that prompted us to move into central London. We decided to move all three kids into the American School and find a new place to live. After looking at several places, we found a townhouse in Saint John's Wood, which was walking distance of the American School and close to public transportation.

Although this meant a forty-minute commute each way to the office, it provided for a more stable family situation. One major benefit for me was its closeness to Heathrow Airport (especially given my travel schedule) along with access to all the cultural and entertainment venues London had to offer. Being close to the Tube was a major enabler to move about the city, we used it constantly, and it provided my older kids mobility without needing a driver's license and car.

One of the big sets of cultural advantages we now had were the museums, with my favorites being the British Museum, the National Gallery, and Churchill's War Rooms. The British Museum housed the Rosetta Stone and the Parthenon Marbles, a collection of ancient Greek sculptures from the Parthenon. They also have a famous statue of the goddess Venus that bears a striking resemblance to the Redhead. Maybe the Japanese had been right about her all along.

The National Gallery has such a broad art collection that you could spend days without fully taking it in. I became a big fan of the British artists Turner and Constable, and my kids probably enjoyed it mostly because of the scenes filmed there from the

Mr. Bean movies. Because the museum did not have an admission fee, I wanted to go all the time, and I frequently suggested we stop by on Sunday afternoon after lunch. My kids would say, "Dad, not again," but it was such a unique opportunity that we had to take advantage of it. Every time I visit London, I have to stop by the British Museum and National Gallery.

I also became a big Churchill fan, and the War Rooms take you back to World War II. It is amazing how sometimes people, with their many flaws, are put in situations at the right place and right time to accomplish great things. Churchill's earlier experiences, learnings, and, sometimes failures, prepared him for that darkest hour, and the extraordinary challenges he had to take on. Churchill's great admonishment was "We shall never surrender!" something I've taken to heart for all facets of life in seeking to reach my potential and achieve the Dream. During my time in the UK, I also had an opportunity to meet former Prime Minister Margaret Thatcher, the first woman and longest-serving PM of the twentieth century, known as the "Iron Lady" for her strong leadership style. Most contemporary polls in the UK put her as the best Prime Minister after Churchill, all things considered.

Theatre was another major cultural experience, including the West End theatre district (the London equivalent of New York's Broadway) and the Shakespearean Globe Theater replica by the Thames River. The Redhead became an expert in acquiring discount tickets, and we often went as a family, enjoying a broad selection of plays and musicals. My personal favorite was *Les Misérables*, based on the story by French author Victor Hugo (who also wrote *The Hunchback of Notre-Dame*). The musical scores are tremendous, and the story themes are redemption, love, and compassion. I've seen it several times, including the twentieth anniversary show with my mentor, John Hitcham, and feel a personal connection with the plot of fighting through adversity.

My most memorable West End experience was taking my eldest daughter, Claire, to see *My Fair Lady* at a theatre near Covent Garden. It was just her and me with seats in a box near the stage. The play opens with a scene of the Flower Girl, Eliza Doolittle, in Covent Garden, which we had just walked through. We had a great evening and walked home through Covent Garden on a beautiful star-filled night, something I will always remember.

After moving into central London, we began looking for a new local church to attend. We had learned the importance of getting plugged into a local church in every place we have lived. My wife had a great experience at our last church, where she was adopted by the Pargeters, an English couple about our parents' age. They helped our transition into the UK and stayed in touch over the years. Eric Pargeter, a former London Metropolitan policeman, gifted me the shield from his helmet, and it holds a place of honor in my office.

There was a church on Abbey Road near the American School that we decided to visit. On our first trip to Abbey Road Baptist Church, we met the pastor and his wife, Iain and Lucy Batty. He was Scottish, and slightly younger than my wife and me, while Lucy was from Slovakia, a physician, and several years younger.

The congregation was relatively small but very diverse, made up of college-aged students from the English language school the church ran, some immigrants to the UK, some local British folks, and a few expatriates, mostly from the American school. We liked the size and makeup of the church, and after meeting with the pastor and his wife, we decided to join.

We would become very active in the church, with my wife leading the children's ministries and me joining both the church and school boards. Because of its congregational makeup and location, it was very different from a typical suburban church. The church was in a relatively wealthy area with sizable Jewish, Muslim, and expatriate populations, while most of the congregation was of limited means, so the key financial resources were linked to property and building rental income, plus giving from the few expats. Because the church was 150 years old and needed major restoration work, we began looking at redevelopment solutions, which would take years to complete. In the interim, we dealt with the basics, like fixing the heating systems and patching the roof.

One of the things that bothered me was the missing stained-glass window above the church entryway, which distracted from an otherwise classic architectural scene. I had remembered seeing the dove shaped "Holy Spirit" stained glass window at Saint Peter's in Rome and thought it would be a perfect fit. We commissioned a British stained-glass artisan to make a version that fit the circular opening above the entryway, and to complement the window, we had a back light installed that would illuminate the stained glass at night. To this day, that window at night is a beacon of light on Abbey Road in London.

My wife and I also got involved with "Operation Christmas Child," which provided Christmas gifts to kids around the world, sponsored by Samaritan's Purse. The local Ford dealers agreed to act as drop-off points, and we were able to get access to Transit vans to pick up and deliver to the central distribution point for Europe. The photos that we have of joyous kids in Eastern Europe, Central Asia, and the Middle East receiving these gifts warm our hearts. One photo of a grandmother with a young boy wearing the scarves my mother-in-law knitted was worthy, I think, of a TIME magazine cover. My wife has continued this yearly tradition of making up shoe boxes to send to children in need around the world, and I think it's a good example of using a network and resources from the marketplace for the good of others.

Pastor Iain and I had similar interests in sports, travel, food, and a love of music. Because of the church's location, he had developed good relationships with the management at Abbey Road Studios, home of The Beatles, and where many of the major music artists recorded. The famous crosswalk featured in The Beatles classic *Abbey Road* album could be seen from the church, where thousands of tourists came to step across the crosswalk each day.

Abbey Road is a working studio and does not provide public tours, but because of Iain's connections, we were invited to visit and see the studio where The Beatles recorded. When I was standing there, I could not help remembering my time standing in the Motown studios years before. The Beatles had great respect for many of the Motown artists and re-recorded several of their hits, making it a moment of real convergence for me.

London offered a great opportunity as a central location for family travel. As in Paris, we tried to visit something relatively local every weekend and make a longer-distance trip at least once per month. There were a couple of discount airlines that offered relatively cheap flights around Europe, so we used cars, trains, ships, and planes to see a couple dozen countries during our time in Europe.

One year, we made a trip to Italy the week after Easter, when we hoped the crowds would be less. The Eternal City has a rich history as the capital of the Roman Empire and the Roman Catholic Church. We toured all the sites, with the Coliseum and the Sistine Chapel being my favorites.

We also visited Saint Peter's, the largest Christian church in the world and home of Michelangelo's Pieta, the iconic sculpture of Jesus and Mary. As we walked in the rear of Saint Peter's, to our surprise, we ran into Pope John Paul II, who was preparing for a service. He was moving slowly and waving as he passed a few feet from us. It was an unexpected surprise seeing the Polish Pope.

My parents, now experienced international travelers, made a return trip to visit us in London. My mother wanted to visit both Rome and Poland while she was in Europe, and on our trip to Rome, we saw all the sites with them, and I was able to arrange for her to sit near the Pope at a mass.

Unfortunately, when we were getting out of our taxi by the hotel, a couple of people tried to rob my father. My dad, a former Golden Gloves boxer from Motown, reacted quickly with several punches, and the burglars fled the scene. He was a little winded but mostly just angry that someone would try to rob him. George Foreman would have been proud of how he handled himself, I think.

Later in their stay, we flew into Warsaw for a bus tour through Poland, ending in Berlin, Germany. On the trip with us was a group of Jewish New Yorkers who were primarily interested in the key Holocaust sites and seeing the Warsaw Jewish ghetto.

Most of the New Yorkers were in their seventies or older and had been directly impacted by the Holocaust, all having lost family members. One of the women on the tour had been whisked out of Warsaw as an infant and never saw her family again. As you can imagine, emotions ran high for my fellow travelers.

Because we had a lot of time on the bus, I developed friendships with several members of the group. Given that I and one woman were the only people under fifty, some of the guys viewed me as a kid, asking me what I planned to do in life. All told, this experience provided me with real-life insight into things I had only read about in history books and helped me to connect personally with people whose backgrounds were so different from mine.

London was a popular place for visitors, and we hosted many family members and friends. We continued our trips with our friends, the Duncans, doing a father and son trip to Scotland, where we stopped to see Stirling Castle, of Robert the Bruce and *Braveheart* fame, while our wives and my daughter headed to the Lake District to take in the beauty and visit the scene of Beatrice Potter's inspiration.

On the morning of our return from another car trip to the continent, on our way back from the original Legoland in Denmark, our friends were robbed of their money and passports in Amsterdam. This put us into crisis mode, and we tried to work with the US Embassy to get new passports. Somehow my friend convinced the UK customs officer to let them on the car ferry with a promise of getting the passports upon arrival. We were the last ones on the Ferry as they pulled up the ramp, and it was a night of celebration as we headed back to the UK. Upon arriving at the port in Newcastle, no one checked for passports, and we drove back to London, elated.

We had another special visitor in our friend Larry, who is blind and had attended the Michigan School of the Blind with Motown artist Stevie Wonder but did not let that limitation stop him from leading an active life. I used to visit Larry with my new company car each year to give him a ride. One time I had a new Mustang convertible, which Larry spent twenty minutes walking around, touching the contours of every body panel. We went to all the sites around London, and people were very accommodating. At the British Museum, they allowed Larry to touch several of the artifacts. At Saint Paul's, we got to go to the front of the line and touch the scale model of the cathedral.

Larry always liked to take pictures for his family, which often resulted in some strange angles. He used a white cane and moved around at amazing speed. Somehow, whenever we were walking together, the cane would end  up between my legs, which I think he did on purpose. All things considered, this was likely a once-in-a-lifetime trip for Larry.

The biggest event during our time in London was the birth of our "English Rose," Rose Elizabeth Cramton. Although it was ten years since we had our last child, my wife and older kids thought we should have another. It was my mother-in-law who said that having my wife when she was thirty-nine years old "kept her young," and it hit a chord with me. We decided to go ahead and take the chance, and it has been a real joy—and has, in fact, kept us young. It also created an interesting dynamic with the older kids, who were very helpful in supporting her, and at the same time, it was a little like having a second family with an only child. Although the other kids were exposed to Motown music, Rosie was my star pupil. I would play the Motown catalog as we cruised in the car and quizzed her on each song title and singer.

We were not the only couple to have a child later in life. Tony Blair, the British Prime Minister, and his wife Cherie, at forty-five years old, had just had a son the prior year who was twelve years younger than their last child. On one occasion, my wife even ran into Cherie Blair at Heathrow airport with baby Rose and had a chance to share with her how she was an inspiration for us.

Within a few months of Rosie's birth, we experienced the impacts of the 9/11 attacks. It was in the early afternoon in London when the attacks began in the US, so I was at the office and the kids were at the American School. Because the school educated the children of many high-profile people, security immediately locked down the buildings, with no access in or out, and it was only hours later that we were able to get our kids. The school would quickly add top-notch security protection, rumored to be ex-Mossad special forces personnel, to protect the students, faculty, and facilities.

Many students at the school had parents who traveled often to New York for business. The father of one of my son's friends was running from the World Trade Center as it was collapsing, his clothes covered in soot and ashes. Air travel was suspended for a period of time, stranding several of the parents in New York. Later, once international travel reopened, Faye made a trip back to the US to see her mother and show her the new baby. There were only a few people flying on the jumbo aircraft she took, out of uncertainty and fear for their safety. Air travel would never be the same.

A few months later, we began looking to go back to the US. Although we were not fearful for our safety, we had been gone from the US for many years. My wife's parents were aging, and with a new baby, she was looking forward to getting back home to Motown. My eldest son and I had grown fond of London and could easily have stayed another few more years, but it was a family decision.

Planning the move back had the same complexities as the process to go over. The key again was finding the school and the house that worked for the family. Because we had sold our house when we left to go overseas, we could not go back to the same place, and had to find a new home for our expanded family.

My wife had grown accustomed to living in a neighborhood with access to shopping and restaurants. There were a few areas near Motown that had both good schools and European-style walkable neighborhoods. We eventually found the perfect place in a suburb just west of Detroit. It was a Victorian-style house located on the mill pond that was originally used to support the area's early industries, including lumber and grist mills. More recently, it supported the hydroelectric system at the local Ford plant built by Henry Ford in the 1920's as part of Ford's village industries. The plant has now been converted into a fitness center and the land around it is a historical village.

As we packed up our London Townhouse, it was clear that the family and I were forever changed by our great adventures in

Europe. We built new and long-lasting relationships, including bringing back a new addition, experiencing new things, visiting new places, taking several smart, measured risks, and being active players in the world around us—taking advantage of the unique opportunities we had been given.

PART 4

GOING PRO – THE WORLD OF PRIVATE EQUITY

After spending a couple of decades in Corporate America, I had the opportunity to "Go Pro" and join the world of Private Equity (PE). Much like professional athletics, Private Equity is laser-focused on winning in the near-to-intermediate term. The role of leadership is geared toward building your team and getting it focused on the key metrics of success, much like professional coaches and managers do for sports franchises. The reward structure is similar to athletics, with substantial rewards for success and little patience for lack of progress. One of the major benefits of the world of Private Equity is that owners, managers, and key employees all have common objectives and metrics.

Team development and relationship building are critical, and key executives will often work together in several different companies, similar to professional athletics, where coaches and players can move from team to team over time. Also, like professional sports, in the world of PE, player performance and merit drive rewards and future opportunity. This fast-paced performance-based environment is definitely not for everyone, but for those that like a challenge, embrace calculated risks, and lean into the pressure to perform, it can be very interesting and rewarding. The next three chapters (12-14) highlight my experiences and the lessons I learned going pro as a global executive working in the high-flying world of Private Equity.

CHAPTER 12
FLYING AROUND THE WORLD

"FLYING HIGH IN THE FRIENDLY SKY" - MARVIN GAYE

I took over the Ford global business development role when we returned to the States, which included managing mergers, acquisitions, and divestitures, along with strategic partnerships and the corporate venture capital investments. The company was continuing to invest in new technologies and expand in Asia while at the same time divesting non-core businesses to raise cash.

During this time, we were trying to manage the family transition, to mixed results. My wife was happy to be closer to her family and our support network, especially with aging parents and a new child. My middle kids seemed to transition easily back into the US system, but my oldest son, now an incoming junior, struggled the most due to starting mid-way through at a new high school. It didn't help that he didn't initially have a driver's license. When my wife suggested he ride his bike around, he was saddened and reminded of his old London life.

We did not fully realize the impact of moving my son from an environment where he had friends with similar backgrounds and unlimited access to move around one of the world's greatest cities to another place where his life experience was so different from his new classmates.

This is not an unusual reentry experience for expats and their families. It's also the reason many expats do several assignments abroad, because they like the excitement of the lifestyle and find the transition back to normal life difficult. It reminded me of friends who returned to Texas from Europe, and all their friends seemed to talk about was their new pickup truck—no one was interested in their adventures. Although I liked pickups, especially the Ford trucks that paid my salary, I was changed by our overseas experiences, and it expanded my interests and worldview into new dimensions.

My son, who had been through many transitions, made the effort to adapt and fit in. He joined the football team, the choir, and later was the lead singer in a rock band. None of this was smooth or totally successful. One of his regrets was not utilizing the English accent he had mastered so well. Ultimately, you must choose to get in the game and try to move forward, or you'll end up on the sidelines.

Shortly after returning to the US, we experienced a family tragedy: The unexpected passing of my father at age sixty-seven from a heart attack on my mother's birthday. Given that it was unexpected, we were all in shock and attempting to cope for a time. The only comfort was that we had seen him that day and everyone was around to support my mother. These events reminded us that everything is temporary, and we need to take advantage of the opportunities we have with our families and the people we love. It makes the other things in life seem so unimportant.

My mother seemed to be coping as well as could be expected, thanks to her support network. She immersed herself in her work at the church and her many ministry activities, especially singing at senior homes. My brothers visited her daily, since they worked at our old high school. We involved her in our family activities, and she had a good group of friends, especially her prayer group that helped her through this difficult time.

About a year later, I decided to take my mother on a trip to celebrate her birthday and take her mind off the anniversary of my father's passing. I wanted to take her to a monastery south of Dublin named after Saint Kevin, the Irish saint that was my namesake. The monastery had been on the pilgrim trail for Irish Catholics for a millennium. After flying into Dublin and enjoying a few days in the Irish capital, we headed to Saint Kevin's.

The topography of the area is incredible, ranging from the rocky desolate area of the Wicklow mountains to a lush valley with a beautiful lake and vegetation. We stayed at the hotel by the monastery and enjoyed a couple of days walking around the scenery; I still have a photo of my mother in prayer with her hand touching the wall of the ancient monastery. At Saint Kevin's, I acquired one of my prized possessions, a gold Irish-style cross that I wear around my neck. The trip was a great time of bonding and healing for both of us.

It was a busy time at work, and my range of activities was very broad. The company was making several technology investments including Sirius Radio, electric and hydrogen technologies, and holographic imaging. At the same time, we were looking at investments and partnerships in Asia, with an emphasis on China and southeast Asia.

I also spent a significant amount of time working on divestitures of non-core businesses. One of the most memorable was a traditional components business that was part of Henry Ford's early vertically integrated manufacturing operations. We had identified a potential Chinese buyer for the multiple-plant operation. The CEO, one of the richest business-people in China, traveled with his staff to visit the facilities. We met in the lead plant conference room with the plant management and UAW union leadership present.

Prior to the start of the meeting, the Chinese CEO walked around the conference room looking at the information boards on the walls. He stopped for several minutes, looking intently at the UAW logo on the wall. After sitting down, his assistant asked if the CEO could make some opening remarks. He began by saying, through his interpreter, "Communism started in Europe with Marx and Engels, came to Russia with Lenin, and China with Mao, and then to America with the UAW. I'm a Communist, you're a Communist, and we will get along well." After he finished, the room was silent, which seemed to last for several minutes. It quickly became clear that his perceived point of connection was lost on his audience.

During the tour of the facilities, he concluded that the relationships between plant management and the communist labor unions which he was familiar with were very different. He concluded that trying to run these facilities in the way he did in

China was probably not going to work, and he dropped out of the purchase process.

Though things didn't work out as expected for the Chinese CEO, his attempt to develop a connection and assess the cultural fit led to the best decision for his company. Sometimes, not doing something is the best decision, instead of trying to force things that don't fit.

The largest and most impactful transaction of my career was the sale of Hertz, the rental car company. We went through a dual-track process, which included filing for an initial public offering (IPO) of Hertz shares while at the same time offering the company for sale to Private Equity firms and then selecting the best outcome. It was a great learning experience for me, both the IPO and the PE auction processes. Because of its size and brand name recognition, there was tremendous interest in Hertz.

During the process, I had an opportunity to meet the world's most prominent Private Equity firms. We received very attractive bids from several PE firms. Given the public sale process would take several years to realize the full proceeds from a sale, we opted for a private equity sale for the whole business. The winning bid was for $15 billion, the second largest leveraged transaction in history at that time, behind the famous RJR Nabisco deal featured in the book *Barbarians at the Gate*. This was a great outcome, and much better than we had expected.

After the transaction closed, I was approached by several of the Private Equity firms about working for them. They liked the combination of my M&A Transaction experience as well as my time working in various operational assignments all over the world.

My wife and I went through an assessment process, comparing the pros and cons of the opportunities versus remaining with Ford. I also talked to my key mentors and advisers about the various alternatives. Finally, my wife and I prayed that we would get clear direction and peace on this decision. We concluded that taking the private equity role was a smart risk, and I accepted a position as Managing Director with a well-known New York-based firm with an international portfolio. It was my first PE experience, and I had the opportunity to work with Tom Stallkamp, a seasoned executive and former President of Chrysler Group. I traveled often, as the firm had offices in the Rockefeller Center Complex in New York, Brussels, Belgium, and Tokyo. My role was to assess new opportunities, serve on selected boards, and assist the portfolio companies as needed.

One of the early potential opportunities we looked at in my new role was the acquisition of Jaguar Land Rover from Ford. We hired my former boss, who had been President of Ford and had previously run Jaguar. Our competition included another group with a former boss of mine who had been CEO at Ford. The third finalist was Tata, an Indian conglomerate that owned a small auto company.

After a detailed evaluation process, we made a substantial bid for the business. The feedback was that we were close to one of the other bidders, but one bidder stood out, and they entered exclusive negotiations to purchase the company. We later found out that Tata had bid a large premium over us and the other bidder. Clearly, Tata believed they could execute a plan to create significant value beyond our assessment. Usually, it's best not to chase things unless you are highly confident you can execute; otherwise, it's not a smart risk.

Shortly after starting my new role, I joined the boards of two of the portfolio companies. One was a German-based auto supplier, where I served on the Supervisory Board—a board in which half the members were elected by employees. This type of co-determination can make reaching an agreement on major decisions a challenge. After joining the board, I led the acquisition of a Madrid-based company to get access to a North American low-cost manufacturing source (LCC) in Mexico. This was my first major foray into Mexico, and I didn't know at the time that it would be a significant experience for my future endeavors. The other board I joined was a publicly held Asian automotive supplier headquartered near Tokyo and traded on the stock exchange.

The PE firm also had an Asian automotive electronics business headquartered in Tokyo that was struggling. Because of my previous experience, I was tasked to make an assessment on whether or not the business could be turned around. After spending a few weeks doing a detailed analysis and developing a potential action plan, I presented to the firm's CEO that I thought the business could indeed be saved. To my surprise, he said, "Ok, and now you can go run it."

This was the beginning of my second assignment in Japan, after my previous experience with Mazda. I was appointed Executive Chairman and had a team of Japanese executives in their late fifties and early sixties working for me. Japan was different from my first experience in the country more than a decade before. Previously, young Japanese people would be dressed similarly with common traditional haircuts and uniforms. This time, when

I was walking around Tokyo, I was surprised at how closely they now looked and dressed like Japanese Americans in California. My conclusion was that the internet and speed of communication had made the world a global village, with trends spreading quickly across geographies. I also noticed more professional women in the workforce, likely a result of more progressive thinking and the shrinking labor pool, which required greater use of the available talent.

To turn the business around, several things were required, including restructuring our bank debt, renegotiating pricing with our customers, and making operational improvements.

The first step was developing an operational improvement plan that could be used to convince lenders and customers to support the business. Although the company had excellent engineers and manufacturing capabilities, it had no hard data regarding its profitability by product or facility. Once we found those numbers, the road map for improving the business became clear. We had three fundamental issues:

1. Several product lines were at a loss due to customer price reductions without offsetting cost reductions.
2. Certain high-cost Japanese and US facilities were losing money.
3. No effort was made on working capital management, especially huge amounts of inventory to protect against potential production issues.

To execute the improvements, we needed some help from our key stakeholders. The first trip was to the banks to get some near-term relief on payment terms and covenants. Once we demonstrated a repayment plan to the banks, they agreed to give us relief. We then visited our largest customer, Nissan, where we were involved with almost all their products, so our success was in their best interest. That's why I ended up sitting across from Yasuhiro-san at that conference table in Nissan headquarters.

We soon developed a joint plan with Nissan to provide some selective price increases and support design changes on products we were losing money on. We rationalized working capital and began targeting inventory levels consistent with a just-in-time business. Finally, we looked at closing some high-cost Japanese and US facilities while moving more product into our low-cost facilities in Thailand and China. Working with the team, these improvements were executed over an eighteenth-month period, substantially increasing profitability and cash flow, and enabling us to reduce debt.

The team was all business during the day and only let their guard down when we went to dinner. It was interesting to hear the perspectives of executives who were the sons of World War II veterans. They had great respect for America's Greatest Generation, who went through the Great Depression and the soldiers who won World War II. Furthermore, they were amazed at how the US treated Japan after the war and helped them rebuild their economy. At the same time, they were worried that the younger generations in both Japan and the US lacked the same discipline and willingness to sacrifice.

During that time, I was traveling to operations all over the world, making several around-the-world trips from the US to Asia to Europe and back again. Neither my wife nor kids were with me on this assignment, and I was living in hotels. I became one of Delta's top global fliers, and because of this, the pilot would come and shake my hand, and I often had a car waiting for me on the tarmac to take me to the terminal.

I then joined the advisory board of a Ukrainian oligarch, who was looking to diversify his investment holdings. For our first meeting, I flew to Kyiv and went over to his office. The security to get through to his office was incredible, like getting into the gold reserves at Fort Knox. Once I got in, he wasn't there yet, so I looked around, trying to find a potential point of connection. The office was large, with wood paneling and leather furniture like something Churchill would have owned. On the walls were several Impressionist paintings; originals, not prints like mine. I said to myself, "This might be my point of connection."

After he entered, we started with the standard greetings, and then I remarked about his Impressionist paintings. I told him that I once had an office near Paris where Monet and Renoir painted in Plein Air. My instincts were correct, and he went on to tell me how he built a replica of Monet's Giverny garden with a Japanese Bridge and water lily pond at his estate outside Kyiv. From this point of connection, we began to build a relationship in which I served on his advisory board, met his wife and father-in-law, a former President of Ukraine, and visited his vacation estate.

During my travels to Europe, I usually stopped in London and visited friends. One of my favorite places was the Ritz Hotel, where I would meet my friend Iain. We often ran into celebrities like former President Bill Clinton and former Prime Minister Margaret Thatcher, who sat at the table next to us at lunch. My favorite hotel to stay at in London was the Lanesborough, and on one occasion, I was sharing a floor with Michael Jackson, the Motown icon and "King of Pop," along with his family. His kids were often out in the hall playing, while he was out preparing for his concerts in London.

During this time, we had a lot of activity on the home front. We continued the father-and-son weekends with our rambunctious teenage boys. A highlight was our whitewater rafting trip to West Virginia. The most challenging part of the trip was when our youngest boys kept taunting the guide, Chas, to see if he could throw us out of the raft. We spent a lot of time in the water because of their behavior, and only the younger boys thought it was funny.

The last big trip was out in the Southwest, where we visited Phoenix, Las Vegas, and the Grand Canyon. My kids, because I would not let them hang over the canyon's edge, say they never "saw" it. Now when I read about someone falling off the canyon, I send them all a group text explaining how their lives were saved by my efforts.

My eldest son completed high school and college and then moved to L.A. to pursue a career in Hollywood. At his graduation from the University of Michigan on a cold April day, he told me he was going to California and wouldn't have to scrape ice off his windshield ever again, and he's been good on his promise so far.

On many of my trips back from Asia, I would stop in to see my son in L.A. My favorite place to stay was in Santa Monica near the Pier. I loved getting up early with jetlag, walking to the pier at sunrise, and looking out at Malibu. I would stop to get a coffee at McDonalds before I walked to the Pier. Most times, there were several homeless people near the entrance. The area was mostly empty that early, and I often would offer to buy them breakfast, but surprisingly, few were interested in a meal.

My second boy, John (now called Jack), finished high school and joined his brother at the University of Michigan. He was interested in political science and had a couple of internships in Washington D.C. During his second internship, he met the love of his life, the lovely Allison.

Unfortunately, around this time, my mother-in-law, Betty (whom I called BL, for Betty Louise) passed away. My wife and I mourned the passing of this precious lady of great faith who had survived three husbands. The Redhead had a special bond with her mother, especially as the baby girl of her family. I always loved BL for believing in me and trusting me with the care of her most precious daughter.

During this time, my daughter Claire began dating. This was the first time I had to deal with this type of situation, not having had any sisters. Claire had found the love of her life, Trevor, in high school, but he took a while to fully realize it. She went off to the University of Michigan, where Jack and Trevor were roommates. We got to know Trevor, and we welcomed him into the family by giving him the nickname "Boots," after his affinity for wearing them.

During college, their relationship blossomed, and upon her graduation, they were married. Pastor Iain came in from London to perform the ceremony wearing his traditional Scottish Kilt. I teared up a bit as I walked her down the aisle. I had taken some dancing lessons to not embarrass myself, and we had a touching father-daughter dance to her Motown song, "Isn't She Lovely," by Stevie Wonder.

Back in Japan, the business had made substantial progress and was making record profits. The firm decided that now was the time to sell, so we began a sales process. After several months, we agreed to a deal with a large European company that was looking to expand its Asian presence. We were pleased with the final financial terms, which made the turnaround a major success, and I headed back to the US very happy for a much-needed vacation. As I boarded the plane back, I had no idea what was about to happen.

Two days after heading back to the US, I was alerted of a major earthquake and tsunami in Japan. Initially, it was difficult to get information as we tried to reach our team in Japan. It quickly became apparent that there was a risk of a nuclear catastrophe at the Fukushima facility, and people were evacuating Tokyo.

On the day of the earthquake, many of our employees were still in the office or plants. Those who lived an hour away by train slept in the office until the trains were running again a day or two later. Amazingly, none of our plants had any significant damage, and our employees were able to return in the next few days to clean up, though it was several weeks before I could get back into the country. When I arrived, I was shocked by how empty and quiet Tokyo had become. I went around to see the facilities to assess any damage and carried around a Geiger counter to alert us of any presence of nuclear radiation, especially at the facilities closest to Fukushima.

We kept the buyer informed on the business but feared they would try to walk away. Given that the reports continued to be favorable on the reduced nuclear risk and that the facilities appeared to not be impacted, we re-engaged with the buyer. The buyer conditioned moving ahead on an independent assessment of the facilities, including no radioactivity within the buildings or inventories. We kept our fingers crossed, and the facilities passed all the tests. Although it was a few months later than originally expected, the buyer thankfully closed on the purchase.

After the sale was completed, the firm put together a team to look at the potential acquisition of the General Motors European company, Opel. We were in a bidding process against a company funded by a Russian bank controlled by Putin. The politics were very complicated, with some concerned about a potential sale to a Russian-backed company. Our firm was worried about security and discouraged the use of texts or mobile phone conversations regarding the transaction to avoid their potential interception. In the end, GM pulled the sale and later sold the business to a French-based automaker.

Around this time, the firm decided to change strategy and was looking to sell off its industrial portfolio and focus on financial services-related businesses, including the other industrial companies where I served on the board. This strategy change prompted me to begin to look for new opportunities.

As I began to look at other potential opportunities, I received a call about a potential executive position at SpaceX. I flew out to California to meet with the management team, who were literally rocket scientists. At the end of the day, I had the chance to meet with Elon himself. After the meetings, I went through an assessment process regarding the opportunity, and although the company seemed very interesting and on the cutting edge, I concluded it likely was not the best fit, and my family wasn't interested in another move at the time.

Shortly after meeting with Elon, I was approached with an opportunity to be the CEO of a turnaround situation for a firm that had purchased several companies out of bankruptcy during the financial crisis. The challenge was to assess which of the companies had the attributes for long-term viability. For each of the companies, I went through the same evaluation process we used with the Japanese turnaround I had just completed. I partnered for the first time with an experienced CFO, Kevin Bagby; we became known as K1 and K2, and would work together several more times in the future.

Some of the companies had potential but either had products that were losing money and/or had been chronically under-invested in by previous owners. It became clear that we needed assistance from our customers to have a path to viability. This led to some interesting negotiations because of the customer-supplier dynamic, which can be adversarial at times, and with the customer usually in the position of power.

In this case, we needed our customers to collaborate with us for a successful outcome. One of the customers was a very large German firm who liked to make us show up early in the morning for day-long sessions. The negotiating sessions seemed to be a psychological battle of wills, with our customer trying to establish their dominance. After a couple of hours of talks, they would ask us if we needed a break, which was a test, and to the Germans, it was a sign of weakness if you needed to pause. On the first day, we had been drinking coffee all morning, and we needed a break.

To turn the tables, the next morning, neither myself nor my team had any coffee. At the usual time for a break, we said, to our hosts' surprise, that we wanted to continue our negotiations. This became a major problem for them since they were all smokers, and they began to fidget for their nicotine fix. They were forced to ask for a break, which gave us a major psychological victory.

Later that night, we joined them for dinner. After a few drinks, my German colleagues were telling us how great Germany was compared to the US. Given that they were the customers and our company the hosts, we tried to just let this go, but after a while, it became tiresome. I told my German colleagues that I had a great uncle who loved Germany and spent a lot of time there during the war driving around. I said he was pretty famous, and they might have heard of him. They asked his name, and I said, "George Patton." They were stunned, and this quickly ended any more talk of German superiority. Ironically, this dinner was a breakthrough and resulted in them no longer attempting to dominate the conversation or making unreasonable demands.

During this time, I was approached about another CEO opportunity for a large auto aftermarket supplier. My wife and I went through our standard evaluation process, including talking to people who knew the company well, and we decided to go on the road again to pursue another adventure.

These first assignments in the Private Equity world allowed me to leverage many of my previous experiences and, at the same time, develop new skills, especially the ability to quickly analyze and develop plans to improve a business. It was surprisingly similar to a new coach coming in, selecting a staff, and putting together a team to execute a winning strategy.

CHAPTER 13
ROCKY

"FIGHT THE POWER" - THE ISLEY BROTHERS

For me, Philadelphia has always been the fighting city, from the time of the American Revolution to the story of Rocky Balboa. When we accepted our new assignment in Philly, we probably should have known that the job wouldn't be accomplished without a fight.

We packed up our house and headed to the birthplace of America. This time, we rented out our house near Motown and initially rented a place in the Philly area along the Main Line, which was named for the famous regional train line running into the city. We lived relatively close to Valley Forge, where General George Washington camped one hard winter during the Revolutionary War.

In Philly, history is all around you, from Independence Hall to the Liberty Bell, to Betsy Ross and numerous museums that make it a special place. The city also loves its sports, with the Eagles, 76ers, Phillies, and Flyers on the professional side, constantly competing for championships alongside the legendary basketball programs at Temple, Penn, Saint Joe's, La Salle, Drexel, and Villanova. Philly is a city of fighters, aptly symbolized by the Italian Stallion, Rocky Balboa. It is a great feeling to run up the stairs at the Philadelphia Museum of Art like Sylvester Stallone did in that iconic scene from the first Rocky movie.

For a city of such great historical significance, Philly, like Rocky, seems to have a chip on its shoulder, always with something to prove. Maybe it's because, over the last two hundred years, America's founding city has been eclipsed, first by New Year City and, more recently, by Washington D.C. In that I-95 corridor, Philly is right in the middle between the financial capital of New York and the political capital of D.C. Philly, which was the birthplace of not only the United States but also the Industrial Revolution in the New World, boasting countless factories throughout the region. This manufacturing power was also eclipsed, initially by the major cities of the Midwest, including Pittsburg, Chicago, and Motown, and more recently by low-cost countries like China and Mexico.

I was recruited to join a large Philly-based auto components supplier with a strong family culture as the new CEO. It had just gone through a sale process to a private equity firm, which fell through. The family that owned the company was looking for someone who could improve the business and position it for sale. I did some up-front due diligence to make sure taking this position was a smart risk, including talking to several people in the financial community with knowledge of the company. I concluded that, with the right actions, the company could be successful and made attractive to a potential buyer.

As I continued my analysis, the question was: How did this company, which had been a successful market leader, end up with such major challenges? It became clear that part of the issue was that the fundamental business environment had changed. The company had historically sold its products to a large group of small to mid-sized local and regional companies. Over the previous decade, several large, sophisticated public companies were consolidating the industry, changing the power dynamic in favor of the customer and away from the manufacturer. This included customer payment terms going from sixty days to a year, which required huge amounts of capital and financing costs to support.

The competitor landscape had also changed. The company traditionally had a cost advantage, using a lower-cost, primarily immigrant workforce in Philly. Over the decade or so previous, competitor manufacturing operations had moved to low-cost countries (LCC), including China and Mexico, putting the company at a competitive cost disadvantage. Furthermore, managing operations in these foreign locations requires different resources and skill sets compared to a local US-based approach.

Finally, the company has been very successful at growing its product portfolio and customer base and was the market leader in most of its product categories. It had a strong salesforce whose metrics focused on sales growth and market share. Product profitability was not tracked nor shared with the sales force or Management Team. A major issue was that certain products were very profitable while others sold at a loss, but historically, the focus and incentives were based on sales rather than profitability.

Based on this analysis, it became clear what areas offered opportunities for improvement, but the challenge is always execution. It is usually difficult to get people or organizations to embrace change, especially in an environment or institution with a strong culture. The first step is to make sure metrics and incentives focus on the results you actually want. Because of this, we changed the focus from primarily sales to profitability, gave everyone clear objectives, shared performance measured by those metrics, and linked rewards to achieving those objectives. This is exactly what you see in a professional sports franchise when the key focus is on winning.

As in the world of sports, sometimes you have to bring in new team members to help an organization reach the next level. In Philly, I brought in several new team members, including reuniting with K2 as CFO. The key here is to integrate the new team members with the rest of the organization, which can be a challenge when you are attempting to make changes in strategy and focus. The good news was that we quickly started to get some traction, which was important not only to the owners but also to the lenders. This enabled us to maintain financing access—the lifeblood of a business.

The organization was still primarily Philly-based and, at the time, the largest industrial employer within the city. This position gave us a lot of exposure with city government, including the mayor and city council, along with the local congressional delegation, who we often interfaced with on key matters impacting the business.

To address changes in the competitive environment, the company had begun moving some operations and products to Mexico and had begun importing select products from China. These were good strategic moves, but like sports, execution is key. Unlike multinationals such as Ford, in which management career paths encourage international experiences, this had not been established in our company, so getting the best and brightest to leave Philly for a multi-year assignment in an LCC location was not common. This made it difficult to build integrated world-class operations in these LCC locations.

Because of its importance to our strategy and operations, I was in Mexico every four to six weeks for several days at a time. The facilities were across the Texas border in Mexico. Safety was always a concern, and one time, I watched from our vehicle as a gunfight unfolded between the National Police and local Narcos. On another occasion, the security team had me walk through the border crossing instead of going by car. As I learned growing up in Motown, you need to plan and always have contingencies in place to make sure you are taking a smart risk as you navigate new situations.

The local Mexican management team thought it would be good if I could give a short speech to our several thousand employees there. I agreed, but wanted to give the speech in Spanish. Although I was not a Spanish speaker, I hoped my French language experience would be helpful in preparing me for the task at hand. My team helped write the text, and we went through several practice sessions before I came down to Mexico. To make this the most effective it could be, the employees were broken into smaller groups by facility, so I ended up doing my speech about ten times. After the speeches, I asked for some feedback. My local team said it was very well received, especially to have an American speak to them in Spanish, but some wondered where the French accent came from.

My speeches weren't the only way we tried to build relationships through shared points of connection like language. We attempted to connect in other ways, like holiday events for all employees in which the management team served the employees. Sometimes simple "thank yous" and kindness can go a long way in any environment, especially when someone in management is willing to risk stepping outside their comfort zone to serve.

Another attempt at team building was our giving of employee-recognition awards, which we had local management nominate their team members for. We even had a contest to design the award trophy, which was made from the parts we produced. Once a year, we had an annual Academy Award-style ceremony at headquarters where we handed out trophies to the winners, along with a cash award, and showed a team video. We wanted to consistently demonstrate that the company recognized and valued employee performance.

On the family side, we had a lot going on. My wife again made a good transition and got involved in my daughter's school and the local church. Philly has a big Catholic Community, and we lived near Villanova University. My wife was invited to join a Catholic women's Bible Study, and she agreed to come, even though she grew up Baptist. After some time, she was asked to be a table leader and enjoyed her time there quite a bit. My youngest daughter, Rose, went to a local Christian school and was involved in several activities. She enjoyed theater and ended up starring in

The Little Mermaid as Scuttle, singing and tap dancing around the stage— which she will never live down.

During summertime in Philly, a part of that world is the New Jersey Shore, known by many as "the Shore." Almost everyone we knew went to the shore in the summer, with many families having places there for generations. The various towns and areas along the shore had big differences in ethnic and socioeconomic makeup, each with its own culture and history. These places felt a lot like our European experience, where developing new relationships and getting accepted into the social fabric of the community takes time and effort. It's easy to feel like a fish out of water sometimes, especially when you compare the salty seaside to the freshwater of the Great Lakes near Motown.

It was during our time in Philly that my second son, Jack, married the lovely Allison Meese in Virginia, and within a few years, our first grandchild, Caroline Elizabeth, was born. It was emotional for my wife and me to experience this new stage as the grandparents of a beautiful baby girl! Jack continued to make progress in his career, serving as a congressional staffer and in the Department of Energy and later in an executive role for an industry group.

A little later, my oldest son Nathan got married to the passionate Vicki Higgins, who also attended the University of Michigan film program. They had a destination wedding in Santa Monica, California. Most of my family had never been to California, and they loved the trip to the Los Angeles area. Vicki's mother's family is from Ecuador, so when I learned that the Panama hat made famous by Teddy Roosevelt was from Ecuador, I bought Panama hats for all the guys in the wedding party. This was a big hit with Vicki's family and a way to build a connection point and relationships with our new extended family.

We also celebrated my mother's eightieth birthday with her bucket-list Alaskan cruise trip with the whole family. This was a memorable trip with my mom, my brothers, and my kids, and the start of many family trips going forward. While living in Philly, I would try to visit my mother in Motown and stay at the house. We would reminisce about the old days, and I would get her a McDonald's senior coffee and egg McMuffin for breakfast, and then take her to her favorite restaurant, Plato's, for lunch. I would sleep on the couch, and my mother would often be up checking on me during the night. It is amazing that even as an adult, to my mother, I was still her kid. Since I was her firstborn, she would introduce me to friends as her number one son. I still cherish those precious times staying at her house and sharing old times together. The bond we had was built on layers and layers of connection we had shared with one another over the years, and there is no substitute for that kind of relationship.

Back in Philly, we enjoyed the success of the area sports teams, with the Eagles and Villanova winning championships. The Eagles were especially fun, given the rabid nature of Philly football fans. The company had premium seats for the Eagles games, and aside from watching the team, watching the fans was pure entertainment. As premium season ticket holders, we had a chance to meet members of the team, and I was always amazed at how they handled the constant attention and pressure to win. Clearly, it takes incredible skill and mental toughness to compete at the highest level of anything, whether it's sports or any other profession where you are trying to be the best in the world.

My most interesting experience at the Eagles Stadium (the "Linc") was not a football game, but a Taylor Swift concert. I went with my daughter, my wife, and fifty thousand other women. Unlike an Eagles game, there were no lines to get into the men's room.

As I was living in Philly, my Spartans were on a roll, winning the Rose Bowl, going to the college football playoff, and on the court, the Men's Basketball Final Four. We enjoyed the opportunity to travel to those events, with the trip to the Rose Bowl game and parade an all-time favorite for me personally.

I also had an opportunity to go back and visit the United Kingdom and attend the London Olympic Games in 2012. For me, the Olympics represent the ultimate challenge, with years of training being tested in one fateful moment every four years. Everything has to be right at that one moment in time. Maybe that is why the sports cliché of the "thrill of victory and the agony of defeat" is so fitting, and magnified for Olympic athletes, who have that one moment to shine. My favorite London Olympic experience was watching beach volleyball at a specially built venue near Buckingham Palace.

After living in a rental house for a few years in Philly, my wife wanted to buy a place. We found a house in Saint David's, which was next to the Main Line train station that went into downtown Philly. The house was an Arts and Crafts style designed by the famous Chicago architect George Washington Maher in the 1890s. Maher was a contemporary of the iconic architect Frank Lloyd Wright and during that time was considered to be on the same level as Wright. Most of Maher's houses were designed around a theme, and the house in Saint David's was the "Arch" house, since all the design cues from the entrance, windows, interior rooms, and staircase were inspired by that geometric shape.

The house was near the beautiful campus of Eastern University, which we enjoyed walking around. I got to know the President and was asked to join the board. It was a good experience, although the dynamics are very different from a for-profit business. Within a university setting, there are many different groups that have influence and input into key decisions, including students, faculty, the administration, alumni, donors, and the board. It was an excellent learning experience to come to understand and be able to navigate this different environment. Every organization, business, family, and community has its own culture, which is why finding common points of connection and building relational capital are critical to success.

Back at the office, the business had made substantial improvements, and within three years, the company achieved record sales and increased profitability by four times over the period, enabling the company to pay a huge dividend to the shareholders. Shortly after receiving the dividend, the owners decided they wanted to retain the business instead of selling it. Given that I was brought in to lead a turnaround and sale of the business, this action prompted my departure and my return to working for a traditional private equity firm.

After looking at a few alternatives, I partnered with some of my former colleagues to buy a computer hardware reseller. We went through the detailed diligence process to determine what price to pay and the levers to focus on to create value. I took on the role of Executive Chairman with a primary focus on business strategy and mentoring the CEO and management team.

This approach worked fabulously, and we were able to substantially grow revenue and profitability. A key area of growth was in Cloud computing, where we serviced market leaders like Google. Within two years, we were approached by an interested party and sold the company for a huge return and a significant multiple on our investment. In sports terms, this was a home run.

Next, I joined a Washington D.C.-based private equity firm as an operating partner and began commuting from Philly to D.C., spending a few days in the office most weeks. The office was a block from the White House, so it was enjoyable to walk around and see the sites. Like most major cities, D.C. had a significant homeless problem, with people constantly approaching you for money. As I usually do, I offered to buy them lunch or dinner, but unfortunately, for whatever reason, my experience was almost always the same, with very few takers.

Taking the train into D.C. was surprisingly enjoyable and pretty relaxing versus driving or flying. My house backed up to the Main Line train station, so I could walk out my back door onto the electric-powered train into 30th Street Station in Philly and on to Union Station in Washington D.C. It reminded me of my time in Europe, where I often used the train system to travel.

I usually went in on Mondays and took the local train, since it was less crowded and only a few minutes more. One of our stops was Willington, Delaware, where, on several occasions, Joe Biden (then Vice President) would board and sit a few rows in front of me at a seat near the restroom. There was some visible security, but nothing heavy, and I never went through any security checks. Maybe I was profiled and determined to be low-risk. They served breakfast on the trip, and after my coffee, I would say good morning to Joe on the way to the restroom.

I tried to spend a few days each week in the office, but much of my time was on the road, either looking at potential investments or visiting portfolio companies. During my time with the firm, I joined several portfolio company boards in several different industries, including distribution and trucking companies. My approach to learning about these new businesses was fundamentally the same analytical approach I had used for years. In many instances, my previous functional and general management experiences provided helpful background for these businesses, while learning the business and developing relationships were critical to effectively assist our portfolio companies.

Initially, I was spending time with a heavy equipment distribution company that the PE firm had owned for about a decade, as the company's sales and profit had been relatively flat for several years. Given that I had spent time overseeing auto dealerships for Ford, I saw several common business drivers. Unlike auto distributors, who make significant profits on service, this portfolio company had historically been focused on new sales. Furthermore, the sales incentive structure was driven by commissions on new equipment, with little focus on selling service contracts. Those who have bought a car from a dealer know how hard they push extended warranties upfront.

We made a couple of fundamental changes in modifying the sales focus and incentives to include service, improved the training and efficiency of the service staff, and implemented market service pricing. We also added K2 as CFO to help monitor and drive our efforts. These actions significantly increased profitability and helped position the company for a successful business sale after over a decade of ownership.

After a few years of commuting to D.C. from Philly, we received the news that my oldest daughter, Claire, was pregnant with her first child back in Detroit. My wife made it clear she wanted to be with her and thought this was a good time to go back home to Motown.

Given that I was on the road most of the time, and it was only an hour's plane ride to D.C., we decided that our time in Philly had come to an end. It was an interesting experience, and we had all learned a lot and developed many new relationships. Except for when playing against my Detroit Lions or Michigan State Spartans, I now cheer for the Eagles and Villanova Wildcats. Motown and Philly have that same gritty, fighting spirit, like Rocky, and I continue to be inspired by the culture of both places.

CHAPTER 14
BACK HOME TO MOTOWN

"I'M COMING HOME" - THE TEMPTATIONS

We packed up our house and headed back to Motown. At this time, we did a major expansion to the house and added a pool to better accommodate the growing number of grandkids. My wife, as always, made a quick transition and was quickly networked back in a local church and re-engaged with her friend group.

Shortly after getting back to Motown, our second granddaughter, Cecelia Rose (or Cece), was born, and we were elated, especially because my daughter was living near us. My D.C. son added their second child, James Edwin, the next year, with his middle name after his great-grandfather. We continued this streak of grandchildren with my son Nathan having his first child and our third granddaughter, Alicia Faye, named after her two grandmothers. My eldest daughter had her second child, Frederick Paul (Freddie), named after his paternal grandfather.

Next came my eldest son, who continued a family tradition by naming his son Kevin Thomas, after his two grandfathers. The Cramton boys were on a roll, and my son, Jack, had his third child, Harrison John. My daughter Claire needed to keep up and had a son, Walter Faye, the name being a reference to her great grandfather and her mother, and our latest, Elliot Gerard, born to Jack and Allison, making a running total of nine. I mention all of this because I consider my grandkids to be among my crowning "achievements" in life, and none would be here without the keys to the Dream that Faye and I learned along the way.

I view my role as a grandfather as both providing fun and wisdom. It is a key mentoring role that is very important. Our time together is a good way to build relationships, teach key principles, and enjoy life. I find play and sports to be very effective ways to accomplish these objectives. One of my favorite activities is our wrestling matches, where I use the moves I learned from Motown's *Big Time Wrestling* show, like the scissor hold, half and full nelson, sleeper hold, etc. As they get old enough, grandkids have the privilege of entering the "King Bed Arena" for a match against Grandpa. Other than bonding and having fun, they learn teamwork and the need to work to get free. On one occasion, we even bought wrestling shorts and robes for everyone and made it a big event.

Aside from wrestling, we include several other contests, including "stealing the pillows", "not today" (a term from my Motown youth), where the kids try to get across to the other end of the bed, and the major event, "Bucking Bronco," where they try to stay on Grandpa's back. These games go back a generation to when I played with my four kids. This is the stuff I live for as a grandfather.

We have also turned Halloween into a multi-generational family event. One of our recent themes was "Super Mario." I was "Bowser" and sang to my granddaughter "Peach" while asking my grandson "Mario" for some candy. We started these a generation ago with my kids, in which my favorite role was the "Cowardly Lion" from the *The Wizard of Oz*. Using my karaoke skills, I did an excellent rendition of "If I Were King of The Forest" while walking the neighborhood.

We have recently started playing hoops in our backyard pool. It reminds me of the early days in Motown playing 21 and H-O-R-S-E, and feels like I'm passing something special from my childhood on to the next generation.  I lift the little ones to give them an early slam dunk experience. Bringing a love of hoops to my grandkids is a special joy.

As my children were growing their families, my wife and I decided to adopt a plan of hosting an annual family event in the summer to get us all together outside of the traditional holiday season. We did a combination of cruises to foreign destinations, cottages, and beach houses around the US. One year we rented a house with a vineyard in Sonoma, a flashback to our time in France.

During the Pandemic, we started "Dress Up Fridays" that were themed events for our "Family Unit," which included our kids and grandkids across the street. Our themes included: a 1950s night with 45 rpm rock records, Roman night with

Togas, Spanish night with paella, Indiana Jones night with the famous hat, and James Bond night with tuxedos and evening dresses. These became something we looked forward to during the pandemic quarantine when outside activities were limited. It reminded me of the escapism that Hollywood movies provided my parents during the Great Depression and World War II.

It was about a year after our return to Motown that I lost my mother, and my brothers and I mourned her passing. Aside from being my mother, she was my original mentor who taught and modeled the keys to living a successful life. In my home gym, I still display the motivational *Charlie Brown* style banners she made for me as a kid, my favorite being "When life gives you lemons, make lemonade."

My youngest daughter, Rose, was moving during high school, and faced many of the same challenges as her older brother when we returned from London. She first selected one of the top schools in the state and was pursuing an International Baccalaureate (I.B.) diploma. Although she was doing fine academically, the program wasn't a good fit in terms of the social and activities aspects. She decided to change schools and attend the local highly rated public school, which also had an I.B. program. That fit was a bit better, but building new relationships late in high school is always a challenge.

One of the things we did together during this time was cruise around in the Mustang listening to Motown. She could name the song and artist like no other member of Gen Z, which made me a proud papa. Unlike the Redhead, who was a bit nervous driving the Mustang, Rose enjoyed controlling the wheel.

There is nothing better than driving down the road with your daughter listening to Motown on a summer afternoon.

My baby finished high school with her I.B. diploma and headed off to the University of Michigan. This was the fourth child of mine to attend the university, while my wife and I were Spartans. With all these Wolverines, we have become skilled at co-existing within the intense rivalry between the schools. My wife always liked Ann Arbor, since it was only a twenty-minute drive to see the kids, while East Lansing was more than an hour away.

It was during this time that I tore my rotator cuff playing tennis and had surgery. The surgery was successful, and the plan was for the Redhead to help me during the recovery period. The night after my surgery, my wife took out the dog and tripped going down the stairs, suffering major injuries including breaking her collarbone. She was rushed to the hospital by ambulance, and I sat there in the waiting room with my post-surgery arm in a sling. There are some things you can't plan for.

My daughter came in from Ann Arbor and drove both of us home early in the morning after my wife was stabilized. She stayed with us for over a month, getting up during the night to get us ice and pain medication. My daughter later told us she knew the day of taking care of us would come, but she thought it would be a few decades in the future. My wife ended up having successful surgery and I healed relatively quickly, and I'm now back on the tennis court.

Toward the end of her college years, Rose was able to study abroad in London, the place of her birth. My wife and eldest daughter had an opportunity to join her at the end and had a great time together enjoying the city. As she was ending her college career, I asked if she felt cheated or wanted to stay on another year and I found her response interesting: She wanted to turn the page and start something new, a mature and healthy response after going through a few very tough years.

She graduated with her degree in economics and headed to D.C. for her first professional job. It was a big transition for my wife and I to be empty nesters, but we were comforted by the fact that she made it through college and was close to her older brother, who lived in the D.C. suburbs with his family.

On the professional side, I began spending time with a couple of our trucking companies. These businesses were very sensitive to economic activity and were struggling to find and retain drivers. One of the real-world issues was to find drivers that could pass the drug tests to meet the Federal requirements to drive these large vehicles. With the advent of legalized marijuana in many states, finding drivers that could pass became a major issue. Matching drivers with available trucks and maximizing utilization was the key to a successful business.

One of our trucking companies had a head of sales who was a former college football player and coach in the SEC. Over dinner, I asked him how he approached recruiting: Was he only looking for five-star players? He told me that he had several five-star players who never made it and three-star players who went on to NFL careers. The key thing he was always looking for was high motor, "Go get 'em" guys. Not only in sports but in most other endeavors, you want "Go get 'em" guys and gals on your team. These types of people can be mentored and developed and will strive to reach their full potential and achieve their dreams.

While I was working with our trucking companies, I was asked to take over as Chairman and CEO of one of the auto suppliers we owned. This company had just gone through an unsuccessful process to sell the business and had lenders that wanted to exit. The situation required quick actions to improve the business and attract new lenders. I brought on K2 to join me as the CFO, given his experience with these types of situations. This was expected to be an eighteen-to-twenty-four-month assignment, and then I would move on to board work. We made very good early progress and were on track to achieve our targets, but then the world changed.

We came face-to-face with the worst pandemic in one hundred years. There was no instruction book or Harvard case study to help us guide a business through this type of crisis. In relatively quick fashion, we were shutting down our operations and laying off the employees. We made an expensive humanitarian decision to pay the health care costs for all our employees because we thought it was the right thing to do. Given that we had no new orders, the only alternative to survive was to collect everything that was owed to us from our customers and limit payments to only essential items. K2, as the CFO, led this effort and kept us from insolvency.

The pandemic had a number of collateral impacts, such as supply shortages for plastic resin and microchips that were critical to our products, while school closures limited the ability of many of our employees to return to work, tight labor markets increased costs, employees all over were resigning in record numbers (the Great Resignation), and the instability of customer orders created manufacturing inefficiencies and mismatched inventories. We were so desperate for workers that I asked my wife to join me on the assembly line on a weekend, making parts to support production requirements. Running an efficient, "just-in-time" auto business was impossible given the supply, employee, and customer issues.

While these issues were already difficult enough to navigate, we faced an issue that every manufacturer fears: an environmental incident with potentially significant impacts. It was initially unclear what the potential ramifications could be, so we alerted the various officials and prepared for the worst. This meant closing the facility immediately, impacting our ability to meet customer requirements at a time of rising demand.

At the same time, we were working with outside consultants and environmental experts to determine the actual impact of the event. The great news was that the systems we had put in place captured almost all of the release and there was no environmental damage. Unfortunately, the media, politicians, and activists did not adjust their narrative to reflect the favorable news. The reputational damage was already done and difficult to impossible to undo for some time.

Even though we had received good news on the environmental front, we were still receiving angry calls and threats, and there were protests near the plant. My wife began receiving death threats, with callers telling her the police could not protect her. We alerted the police and hoped this would stop, but we were wrong.

I woke up on a weekday morning to go work out, but as I looked out the window, I noticed that the tires on our vehicles were slashed, our garage spray-painted, and the driveway was marked with environmental slogans.

As I called upstairs to my wife, we heard banging and shouting at the front of our house. I looked outside to see over a dozen people dressed in black like ninjas. One "terrorist" approached and placed explosive projectiles pointed at our house, and then lit them. We immediately began yelling and called the police. The authorities responded quickly, and the ninjas began to run for their cars. Several were caught by the police and arrested. We only found out later that a few of those arrested had been involved previously in eco-terrorism and that the FBI had an Eco-Terrorism Task Force.

The police were worried about additional attacks, so we added armed security. My wife was shaken and frightened, while I remained upset and angry. When I checked in one morning, the security team initially thought they had an incident when a projectile was thrown at the security vehicle, only to discover that it was the paper delivery person with an errant throw.

It is at these times that you learn who your friends are, and a huge multitude rallied to support us. My brothers offered to come over and told me I needed a big guard dog like our days in Motown. I even had a Philly friend who was a security expert drive in to assist. On the other hand, we found that we were "doxed" by people we had known for decades—people we thought were our friends. These people acted maliciously without talking to us or knowing the facts.

Unfortunately, we were just getting over another family tragedy when this happened. My brother Mark (or Sharky), who had been my childhood roommate, teammate, and best man, passed away unexpectedly from a heart attack. Our family, especially his wife and two daughters, were crushed. Given our closeness in age and shared experience, it was like losing a part of myself. We would frequently communicate by text to joke, reference old stories, or debate the news of the day. I still find myself wanting to text him about something that is going on just to get his reaction.

To cope with the personal and professional crisis during this period, I leaned heavily on my relationships with Faye, family, good friends, and mentors. I also had a strong spiritual support network through my church and men's group.

At the same time, I found getting away can be great for mental health, and for me, travel and sports are great outlets. My friend Tim is a big NASCAR racing fan and had relationships that enabled us to meet some of the teams, racers, and celebrities. Going to the Daytona 500 and Talladega for races was a blast, especially when a friend's team finished in a surprising second place.

One of my bucket-list items was driving Route 66, the famous road from Chicago to L.A. that was memorialized in the iconic song by Nat King Cole. Through Tim's cousins, we were able to drive a reproduction 1969 Shelby Mustang GT 500 Convertible. The car was "Grabber Blue," and the dashboard was signed by Carol Shelby himself. We picked it up in Saint Louis and drove it all the way to the end of the route at the iconic Santa Monica pier. Going through all the towns along the way was like stepping back in time to the 1950s. You also get a sense of the diversity of topography and people in our country as you go from the Mississippi River across the plains, through the desert, and to the coast. I highly recommend the trip to every adventurer and car lover.

I loved this trip and the car we drove so much that I had Duncan Brothers Customs build one for me. They did a magnificent job, and the car has been featured in various publications, shown at SEMA, placed second at Autorama, and had its own episode on the *Big Kenny's Crank It Up Garage* TV show. To quote Big Kenny from the Country Group "Big and Rich," the car is a "piece of art!" (The front cover features a picture of this beauty.)

One of my favorite places outside of Motown is my wife's cousin John's cottage in Bancroft, Canada. It has been in the family since the early 1960s, and staying there is like being in a window into the past. The place still has a rotary dial phone with a party line (a shared landline). Cell phone coverage is spotty, and there is no Wi-Fi, which my wife thinks is perfect. The TV has a VHS and DVD player to watch TV shows and movies from the 1950s and 1960s. My favorites are *The Twilight Zone* and *The Munsters*.

Motown is the only large American city that lies North of Canada, while the Canadian city of Windsor is across the Detroit River. The town of Bancroft is an eight-hour drive from Detroit and is located north of Toronto in cottage country. This little village is called the "Mineral Capital of Canada" and is anchored by a Tim Horton's restaurant, the Canadian McDonald's. As you might expect, Tim Horton was a Canadian NHL Hockey player for twenty-four seasons who got into the restaurant business. The place is always busy, and the parking lot has the best cell phone reception in town.

After getting your fishing license and worms at Canadian Tire, a smaller version of Walmart, you're ready to get on the lake. The ride from the main road to the cottage is over a mile on a rocky and hilly unpaved road, perfect for my Bronco sports utility vehicle. There is a legend in the family of "Betty's Hill," in which my mother-in-law was unable to conquer the trip up in her Lincoln Continental. She was forced to leave it at the bottom and walk up.

My first trip to Bancroft was the summer we were married, and we have tried to come back every year, as often as possible. We have gone through all stages of life at the cottage, from being newlyweds, to married with children, and now happy grandparents. This is a special place where family relationships are strengthened in a slower and less stressful environment. Everyone needs a bit of Bancroft from time to time to get away from the fast pace of life.

Back at work, we got through the environmental issue, but it had a lingering impact on the business. Given that our main plant was shut down for about a month, we fell behind on customer orders and began to work 24/7 in an attempt to catch up. Although we made some progress, it was a slow process, and our people were exhausted from the pace. This increased absenteeism and turnover while stressing our systems and financial resources.

At the same time, I was approaching four years in the position, way beyond the amount of time expected and near the maximum time agreed. The firm was able to identify my replacement and I retired as CEO while remaining on the board for a period of time. My wife was elated that I was stepping back from the long work weeks after several decades and now focusing on my board and consulting work. This decision enabled me to be more engaged with the family, especially my grandkids. I've also been more involved with some of the other travel and sports activities I enjoy. Taking a step back has provided me the time to do some writing, speaking, and guest lecturing about my experiences.

As I have been traveling during this new chapter, I've had the opportunity to revisit one of my favorite places, to attend a great sporting event, and celebrate the 100th anniversary of a "miraculous" athletic result. I'm referring to the 2024 Paris Olympics, and the anniversary of the track event memorialized in the Academy Award-winning movie *Chariots of Fire*. The main characters of that film are Harold Abrahams, the son of a Jewish banker, and Eric Liddell, the son of a Scottish missionary to China. They were able to adapt to and successfully navigate the challenges they faced to "miraculously" win Gold Medals in the 100- and 400-meters races, respectively, at that earlier Paris Olympics against great odds by exemplifying the key principles outlined in this book. These are the kinds of opportunities and experiences I make sure not to miss in this most recent chapter.

Coming back to Motown has been both an ending and a new beginning. As the Redhead always tells me, life has many phases, and you must enjoy each to the fullest as you pass through them. The keys of investing in relationships, trying new things while aligning your talents and interests, taking smart risks, and being an active participant have been important during each phase, and will continue to be until the end of the journey.

CONCLUSION
HIGHER GROUND

The experiences and lessons I had as a CEO, Executive Chairman, and a member of several boards of directors were the culmination of the kind of successful career that I can only begin to describe as a blessing and an amazing journey. I want to leave you with these final perspectives from the top of the international corporate and PE worlds, combined with what I believe are the Keys to the American Dream. The point isn't to brag or boast but to help you as you climb to the top of your own mountain. At the end of the day, this is what I learned as I took in my own view from the top.

CHAPTER 15

VIEW FROM THE TOP

"AIN'T NO MOUNTAIN HIGH ENOUGH" - DIANA ROSS

In life's journeys, we all travel through highs and lows as we strive to achieve our dreams. My story is no different. Like head coaches and general managers in professional sports, business leaders in the most senior leadership positions of CEO, Executive Chairman, and members of the board of directors have a much different role than division managers and functional leaders. When you are at the top of the "organizational mountain," the focus moves from a narrower area of responsibility to a broader focus on strategy, personnel development, and organizational culture.

During my career, I had the opportunity to be CEO and/or Executive Chairman of five companies and served on over twenty-five for-profit boards of directors, including three publicly traded companies and several non-profit boards.

The primary responsibility of these roles is to develop the strategy of the organization. This is where you can leverage all those prior experiences, both successes and failures, to create a business strategy. This is also why trying different things and taking smart risks, especially early in your life and career, are critical building blocks for these kinds of future key leadership positions.

In these leadership roles, it can be lonely at the top of the mountain, and getting advice and counsel is critical. Since the whole organization or team you are leading watches your every move, it is important to have a sense of self-awareness and have sources from which you can get honest feedback. This is why mentors, close confidants, and support groups are essential to being successful in both key leadership positions and life in general. I have had several mentors throughout my life who have helped advise me on my journey.

One of the most important support groups I have been involved with is the CEO Forum, a group of Christian CEOs from big household-name public companies, large family businesses, and private equity-owned firms. This group offers the opportunity to share with peers, many of whom are dealing with the same issues, and provides a forum to support leaders through both business and personal challenges.

When I became involved in the CEO Forum, I was privileged to be matched up with a top-shelf mentor, Dick Schultz. Dick had spent his career in athletics, first as head baseball and basketball coach at Iowa, and then Athletic Director at Cornell and Virginia, eventually coming to serve as the head of both the NCAA and the US Olympic Committee. He then led the CEO

Forum's efforts in Asia and oversaw our regional CEO Forum group in D.C. He is the most wise and humble senior executive I have ever met—a rare combination. For me, he exemplified the principles of *servant leadership* where listening, empowering others, having a positive attitude, hearing honest feedback, solving problems quickly, leading with resolve, and serving others are key attributes.

During one of our monthly calls, I mentioned how the last few years of the pandemic had been the worst of my career, and that I was tired and weary. As he listened to my tales of woe, Dick responded with a story. He began talking about growing up during the Great Depression and World War II. Dick said that during that time, "We had sixteen bad years in a row, and you know what, we got through it and were ok. You will be ok too." I thought about that perspective, in which he faced the fundamental questions of life and death during that period, while my issues were relatively minor and really just a few short-term inconveniences. Having mentors who can listen and give you a perspective is invaluable at any point in life, but especially in these senior roles, it's a gift to have a real-life Yoda listening and providing advice.

Sometimes, these mentoring and support relationships can work both ways. My friend Pastor Iain Batty and I have had this mutual support relationship since my time in London. We talk often and try to get together a couple of times a year in person, usually once in the US and another time in Europe. On his US trips, he usually combines our time with visits to a few of the expats that have attended his church over the decades. We usually meet someplace warm in the spring to catch up, with Miami being a favorite location. I usually do the return trip to Europe in the summer or fall. We share a long list of common interests, and while I have introduced him to Motown, he has taught me all about The Beatles and other British rockers.

Since we have known each other for decades, it's always easy for us to catch up. Furthermore, since we are not directly involved with each other's day-to-day lives, that distance provides an ability to give new and potentially unbiased perspectives on the issues we face. Developing mutual support relationships that can last over time, like my friendship with Iain, is a powerful practice for long-term health in your personal and professional life.

Furthermore, being a mentor, giving back, and sharing your experience with others is a critical and noble role. I have been working with students and younger professionals to share my experience and help them develop and reach their potential, which is a key focus of this chapter in my life's journey.

As a senior leader, developing your team is one of the most important elements of your role. Like a head coach, you need to make sure you are selecting and then developing your immediate team and that they, in turn, are doing the same with their people. To be successful in leadership, you need to pick the right people, develop them, and delegate clear objectives and responsibilities, then monitor their performance and provide feedback. Like with an orchestra, you need to be the conductor, not the individual performer. Development plans need to be specific to the individual within a clearly defined and communicated framework. Determining the best development and career plan usually requires helping your people to match their interests, skills, and capabilities with available opportunities.

Organizational culture can be the most challenging element of leadership, depending upon the state of the company or enterprise you join. Some companies have a history of strong management, financial stability, and growth potential that only require minor modifications to continue or enhance success. Other companies may have none of those attributes, requiring a complete turnaround or comprehensive rebuilding strategy. Because of this, you need to carefully develop your plan to move the state of the company and its culture to where it can achieve success for all the key stakeholders.

Be it a sports rebuilding or a business turnaround, the process starts with getting the right team in place, equipping and developing the team, and then establishing the identity or organization culture. In these turnaround situations, the team you inherit usually needs to be adjusted to either improve capabilities or to achieve alignment with the new direction. Most turnarounds start with a core of team members hungry to pursue a winning strategy, while another group is usually either unwilling or unable to make a positive contribution and needs to be replaced quickly, and the last group are those on the fence looking for reasons to get on board. This last kind of person is sometimes referred to as "being from Missouri"—the "Show Me" State. If you can get that last group on board, you will have enough of the total organization's support to move forward with momentum and purpose.

To galvanize the organization around a strategy of success, achieving and communicating small victories is critical. Everyone wants to be part of a winner, so demonstrating some successes, even minor ones, is very powerful. Furthermore, recognizing and rewarding your team members is critical to building a winning culture. The universal truth I learned in running companies around the world is that everyone, no matter what country they are from, wants to be respected and appreciated. Tying the reward and recognition system to achieving those team goals is critical to driving success in any endeavor—business, sports, or life.

Speaking of turnarounds, recent initiatives led by the mayor and local business community have resulted in a true Renaissance in Detroit, which is being increasingly recognized on a national level. We hosted Mayor Mike Duggan at the University of Chicago Booth School's annual Economic and M&A Forum, where I have served on the steering committee for over a decade. One of my good friends, Gary Silberg, from co-host KPMG, interviewed the mayor about the tremendous comeback happening in Motown. After the presentation, most of the participants were not only impressed but wished they were seeing the same level of leadership and progress in their cities. It demonstrates what strong leadership and passionate business and community involvement can do. Hopefully, Motown can keep that momentum going forward—and "Keep on Keeping on."

The role of a board member is more like an owner or general manager in sports, compared to a head coach who more closely functions like a CEO. Board members usually have primary oversight responsibility, review, and approve strategies, and provide key insight in areas of expertise. Unlike the head coach or CEO who runs day-to-day operations, the board is much more focused on strategy, oversight and making sure you have the right CEO in place—and that they are developing their team.

I have had several board experiences, including with three publicly traded companies. In many ways, the board role can present a good mentoring opportunity to share knowledge and experience with the management team. Additionally, the same analytical skills and research that you use when evaluating smart risks are also applicable to board roles and reviewing business strategies. This type of *risk analysis* has applications to both business and life in general. Developing a competence in this area is key to navigating through life and adapting to change.

One of the public companies I have served on in a Board role is Helmerich & Payne, a Tulsa-based market leader in drilling solutions and technologies. It has been a great professional opportunity in applying my skills and experience to a new industry. The people are top-notch, and when I visit the oil fields, I feel like I'm rubbing shoulders with the offspring of the pioneers that settled the West with grit, hard work, and a can-do attitude. One of the best things for this Motown kid is that I get to sample barbeque after every Board meeting—and I believe Tulsa has the very best (although my brother-in-law in Austin, Texas, would debate that). Great food is just one perk that comes with embracing a variety of roles and opportunities.

Diversity of experience is very important for those in senior leadership, especially CEO and board roles. On one of the public boards of directors I have served on, the company published a directors' skills and experience matrix for their shareholders. Concretely, the company emphasized background and experience in the following areas:

- Corporate governance
- Diverse industries
- CEO and executive leadership positions

- Global business assignments
- Information technology
- Private equity and capital markets
- Public board experiences
- Risk management
- Strategic planning and analysis
- Financial expertise (which is key for audit committee members)

It's important for you to build your relevant set of experiences and skills that provide value and help you differentiate yourself. As you advance in your career, you should continue to add to your resume skills and experiences that both supplement and complement what you already have learned. Lifelong learning and development are key to success in all aspects of life.

These senior roles have several benefits but come with huge pressure, responsibilities, and accountability. It reminds me of one particular dinner discussion I had with my adult children, who were in the early stages of their careers at the time. The question was what they thought about being a CEO. Although each one had career aspirations and wanted to be successful, they all acknowledged the burdens and commitments they observed in the CEO role while watching their father. My eldest daughter captured the downside by saying, "The problem with being a CEO is that one of your employees can do the dumbest thing in the world, and you are held responsible!" She's right, as President Harry Truman famously said, that for CEOs "The buck stops here."

Given that accountability and responsibility ultimately rest with those in these executive leadership roles, getting the fundamentals right is incredibly important to increase your chances of success. That is why focusing on the building blocks of building relationships and developing a strong team, making sure you have the diverse experiences and skills needed, doing the analytical assessment to assure you are taking smart risks, and finally, striving to be fully engaged and playing to win, are absolutely crucial to playing your best game.

EPILOGUE
STAYING IN TUNE

The major learnings along my journey from Motown kid to Global CEO to today revolve around those four key fundamentals of finding points of connection to build relationships, pursuing alignment in your talents, interests, and opportunities, taking smart risks, and being a player in your life, rather than watching it pass you by as a spectator. This is how you will stay "Tuned," by navigating the course of your life and career and adapting to the changes that will surely come your way. Real life is integrated, though, with family, job, and outside activities interwoven together. In the same way, all of these fundamentals work together and are interrelated with each other. These have been refined throughout my journey and are also, I believe, the keys for you to achieve your potential and live your Dream.

The following is a quick overview of the four keys to be a handy reference.

When it comes to relationships:

- Building relational capital is the basis for long-term relationships.

- Identifying a point of connection is a key tool for initiating relationships—and a critical skill to develop.

- Invest in those deep relationships with family and friends. Do not over-invest in transactional relationships.

- Choose wisely when selecting a life partner.

- Carefully select the people you hang out with; spend your time with positive influences.

- Develop a self-awareness about how you relate and impact others.

- Find good mentors and a support network that can give you helpful feedback and hold you accountable.

- Cultivate a network of relationships in your personal and professional life, which is a critical success factor.

- Be a good teammate and learn to play different roles. Sometimes you lead, while other times you are in a support role.

- Look for opportunities to give to and support others; be a mentor; share your time, skills, and experience.

- The ability to build strong relationships relies on credibility established from your actions in word and deed.

- Remembering that no one does it alone, so acknowledge those relationships that have been key to your success!

- Relationships with family and friends are your real lasting legacy.

When it comes to trying new things:

- Always be curious and seek to learn new things, which will enable you to grow in all areas of your life.

- Try to do things that will get you out of your comfort zone—but don't be foolish; carefully think through risks before taking the leap.

- Explore, test, and align your talents and interests with opportunities to the best of your ability—test drive before you buy.

- Endeavor to understand the differences between careers and vocations on the one hand compared with interests and hobbies on the other—"do what you love" is too simplistic for most people's lives.

- Because you are likely to have multiple careers and vocations, along with various outside interests during your life, you need to be a lifelong learner and explorer to identify the best opportunities to pursue through the various stages of life.

When it comes to taking smart risks:

- Living life to your full potential requires selective risk-taking.
- Do not make important decisions based purely on emotion.
- Develop the ability to benchmark, analyze, and assess pros and cons of decisions prior to making them.
- Seek good advice, counsel, and spiritual guidance as needed from trusted experts, friends, mentors, and support groups.
- Learn to balance risks with opportunities; sometimes not going forward is the best solution, rather than forcing things that just don't fit.
- Become quick to make adjustments as information or circumstances change; learn from your successes, and especially, your failures.

When it comes to being fully engaged:

- You need to be a player, not a spectator, in life.
- Life provides windows of opportunity; don't miss them.
- Everyone has challenges; you will need to push through difficult situations.
- Decide each day whether to be engaged; choosing to be in the game is a habit you have to practice.
- Work to be a positive contributor in all of your endeavors.
- Approach life like a great adventure; this is the story you get to live.
- Living a life of immersion is key for success and achieving your full potential.

Importance of balance

Developing a sense of balance and having a support network to keep you on track is critical. Achieving the right balance over time in the following areas is important:

- Mental, physical, and spiritual health
- Family, job, and outside activities
- Deep friendships, casual connections, and transactional relationships
- Student/learner, friend, and teacher/mentor roles

Like a great Motown song or a perfectly tuned engine, life has a rhythm to it, with different situations and life stages impacting the relative balance of these areas. It is important to develop a sense of self-awareness and have relationships where you can get honest feedback to hold you accountable if you are out of rhythm or balance. Life is a great journey, and navigating successfully along the path and attaining your goals and dreams requires a lot of effort and help along the way.

In the words of my favorite artist, the genius Michelangelo, painter of the Sistine Chapel, sculptor of the Statue of David, and architect of Saint Peter's in Rome, "The great danger for most of us lies not in setting our aim too high and falling short; but in setting our aim too low and achieving our mark."

As I reflect on my journey, starting in Motown, traveling around the world and now back, a final song comes to mind.

Being on the roof, listening to those old Motown records, there is a whole world waiting out there. For me, there's nothing better than seeing the world while listening to those old Motown records. My hope for you is that you enjoy the journey, get your keys to the Dream, and stay tuned!

THE TUNED PLAYLIST TO STAY IN THE GROOVE

SONG	ARTIST	CONNECTION
ABC	Jackson 5	The Early Years
Everybody was Kung Fu Fighting	Carl Douglas	Playing Around
A Ball Of Confusion	Temptations	Change is a Coming
Heat Wave	Martha Reeves and the Vandellas	Soul Awaking
Dancing in the Streets	Martha Reeves and the Vandellas	1968 Tigers
Nowhere to Run	Martha Reeves and the Vandellas	Dave's Song
I'll be Doggone	Smokey Robinson	Scott's Song
I'll be There	Four Tops	Bee's Song
Since I Lost My Baby	Temptations	Lost Boys
What's Going On	Marvin Gaye	Teacher Mentor
Papa was a Rolling Stone	Temptations	Dad's Song
You are the Sunshine of my Life	Stevie Wonder	The Redhead
Love Machine	Miracles	Mark's Song
Ain't Too Proud to Beg	Temptations	First Date
Let's Get It On	Marvin Gaye	Going Off to College
Ain't Nothing Like the Real Thing	Marvin Gaye	Joining Corporate America

THE TUNED PLAYLIST TO STAY IN THE GROOVE

SONG	ARTIST	CONNECTION
I Heard it Through the Grapevine	Marvin Gaye	Nathan's Song
Second that Emotion	Smokey Robinson	Johnny's (Jack's) Song
Power	Temptations	Asian Experience
My Cherie Amour	Stevie Wonder	French Experience
Isn't She Lovely	Stevie Wonder	Claire's Song
Crusin	Smokey Robinson	All Over the Map
You Really Got a Hold on Me	Beatles and Smokey Robinson	United Kingdom Experience
For Once in My Life	Stevie Wonder	Larry's Song
My Girl	Temptations	Rose's Song
Flying High in the Friendly Sky	Marvin Gaye	Flying Around the World
Fight the Power	Isley Brothers	Rocky
I'm Coming Home	Temptations	Back Home to Motown
Enjoy Yourself	The Jacksons	Grandkids Song
Ain't No Mountain High Enough	Diana Ross	View from the Top
Motown Song	Rod Stewart with the Temptations	Epilogue

ABOUT THE AUTHOR

KEVIN CRAMTON grew up in Motown in a family of four boys attending Detroit public and parochial schools. He married his high school sweetheart, the Redhead, Faye, and they have four children and nine grandchildren. Kevin and Faye live across the street from three of their grandkids slightly west of Detroit and just south of the famous 8 Mile Road.

Cramton has served as chief executive officer or executive chairman of five companies and has served on the Board of Directors of over 25 businesses. He has worked in various management positions during a 20-year career at the Ford Motor Company, including global responsibilities for Ford's merger and acquisition activities, executing around 50 transactions with a value of about $25 billion during his career. With assignments in Asia and Europe, including working in 4 world capitals, Cramton has a highly honed global perspective on navigating relationships.

He holds an MBA degree in finance and a BA degree in business administration from Michigan State University and an alumnus of the London Business School Executive Management Program.

www.ingramcontent.com/pod-product-compliance
Lightning Source LLC
Chambersburg PA
CBHW020536030426
42337CB00013B/874